VOLTAIRE

BOOKS BY WAYNE ANDREWS

Pianos of Sympathy (1936)
(under the pseudonym of Montagu O'Reilly)

The Vanderbilt Legend (1941)

Battle for Chicago (1946)

Who Has Been Tampering with These Pianos? (1948)
(under the pseudonym Montagu O'Reilly)

Architecture, Ambition and Americans (1955)
(revised edition, 1978)

Best Short Stories of Edith Wharton (1958)
(editor)

Architecture in America (1960)
(revised edition, 1977)

Germaine: A Portrait of Madame de Staël (1963)

Architecture in Michigan (1967)

Architecture in Chicago and Mid-America (1967)

Architecture in New York (1968)

Siegfried's Curse:
The German Journey from Nietzsche to Hesse (1972)

Architecture in New England (1973)

American Gothic (1975)

Pride of the South:
A Social History of Southern Architecture (1979)

Voltaire (1981)

Draper Hill, *Voltaire.*

VOLTAIRE
Wayne Andrews

A NEW DIRECTIONS BOOK

Manufactured in the United States of America
First published clothbound and as New Directions Paperbook 519 in 1981
Published simultaneously in Canada by George J. McLeod, Ltd., Toronto

Library of Congress Cataloging in Publication Data

Andrews, Wayne.
    Voltaire.
    (A New Directions Book)
    Bibliography: p. 151
    Includes index.
    1. Voltaire, François Marie Arouet de, 1694–1778.
2. Authors, French—18th century—Biography.
PQ2099.A56   1981   848′.509 [B]   80-29565
ISBN 0-8112-0880-1
ISBN 0-8112-0802-8 (pbk.)

New Directions Books are published for James Laughlin
by New Directions Publishing Corporation,
80 8th Avenue, New York 10011

CONTENTS

LIST OF ILLUSTRATIONS

To Goldwin Smith

PREFACE:
THE SMILE IS VOLTAIRE

There are many eighteenth centuries. There are countless interpretations, patiently invented by conscientious historians, of the puzzling development of Europe from the Peace of Utrecht to the French Revolution. Occasionally these interpretations are plausible. To some people, for example, it is plausible to assume that eighteenth-century France was the home of reason: Voltaire has been made the hero of this world where common sense was carried to its ultimate conclusion.

However, the Marquis de Sade makes his appearance astonishingly quickly once Voltaire leaves the scene and the unreasonable French Revolution begins. Perhaps we should begin at the beginning and give Voltaire another chance.

Voltaire has been accused of setting out to do good. This is a serious charge, for doing good has always been the preoccupation of simple minds, and it is really libelous to suggest that he was so uncomplicated. He had a sense of humor, as his century well understood, even though this facet of his character has been overlooked by the serious-minded. As a matter of fact, when he appeared to be doing good, more often than not he was using his fine intellect to amuse himself.

It has also been claimed that he was the very incarnation of tolerance. Up to a point this is a convincing argument. He was

1

tolerant of Catherine the Great: he never joined the critics who pointed out that she only got to the throne by having her husband murdered. And he was also tolerant of Frederick the Great, even though more than one of Frederick's contemporaries wondered if he were housebroken. It is obvious that Voltaire was eager to cultivate all bright and emphatic rulers, no matter what their moral standards. He drew close to them, smothered them with adulation, and certainly enjoyed being near the center of power.

He was also tolerant now and then of the Roman Catholic hierarchy. He was a great friend of the sophisticated Cardinal Bernis, whom Casanova claimed as an ally in his Venetian adventures. He also flattered—or teased—Pope Benedict XIV by dedicating a patently irreligious drama to him. And he was on the best of terms with Pope Clement XIV, who had, it must be admitted, a superlative sense of humor. "Have that heretic come in at once!" he commanded when a Calvinist called at the Vatican. "He must be awfully bored in my waiting room, while the others out there are acquiring the odor of sanctity."

But Voltaire was always intolerant of Christianity. For this all Christians should be thankful. Religion, after all, is never more alive than when under attack. Voltaire did more than his part. And if he could never conceive of the stuff of which faith is made and so never grasp the fascination which religion held and holds, he could allow that others must have their faith. "If God did not exist, we should have to invent Him," he argued.*

He was no atheist but a deist, a member of that strange fraternity that seems to have become extinct in the twentieth century. Tom Paine was a loyal member and so was Jefferson, who took the trouble to edit all references to the supernatural out of the Gospels, pronouncing the result "the most sublime edifice of morality which has ever been exhibited to man." A supreme being was acknowledged by all deists, but revelation was discarded and the supernatural appeal of Christianity denied. Voltaire was one of the most industrious critics of the Bible, revolted by the Old Testament, which he found a tissue of lies, and by the

*Here a footnote may be allowed. The line comes from a scrap of verse, "To the Author of the Three Impostors," dating from 1769.

miracles of Jesus. Getting what appeared to be the facts straight was all important, and he quite forgot that what we believe may be more fascinating than arguing over what actually happened. The William James who pleaded that "we are all such helpless failures in the last resort," reminding us that "the sanest and best of us are of one clay with lunatics and prison inmates," would have been incomprehensible to him.

So if you believe in Christianity, you will never say that Voltaire was tolerant. Was he a poet? This is doubtful, no matter if his contemporaries were impressed by his verse. If poetry may be described as passion spent plus passion corrected the next morning, he was no poet. Pope could be passionate even if vindictive; Voltaire was more likely to be calculating. He also fails as a dramatist, so the twentieth century has decided. There seems to be next to no chance that his plays will be revived. They are, and this is the unforgivable sin, dull when compared to those of Racine or Corneille. All too often he is guilty of preaching on the supposed failings of Christianity. And he lacked, for all his wit, the gentle touch of his contemporary Marivaux.

The tale of *Candide* is his eternal advertisement. But this is unjust. He was one of the supreme historians, and it is doubtful that anyone will surpass his *Age of Louis XIV*. Discarding, as he intended, all unnecessary details, he wrote a defense of Louis that should silence almost all criticism. Like a lawyer protecting a client, he conceded faults but proved that here was a great king, a great patron of literature and the arts.

Not that Voltaire himself was *artistic*. Intellectually he could sympathize with the arts, but he was no collector of paintings, had no instinct for music, and the houses in which he lived were mediocre examples of architecture in an architectural century.

What then is the charm of Voltaire in the twentieth century? If you imagine the eighteenth century to be the era of elegant precision of language, he has the very best claim to represent the age, and his elegant sarcasm will never lack an audience. More important, he was frequently infuriating, and the infuriating are always invaluable. He was the eternal enemy of rust, and since rust is the bane of all societies, he will always appeal to the critical sense.

Here someone may argue that the clock never stopped in the eighteenth century: the elegant precision of Voltaire, founded on the prose style of La Bruyère and the other masters of the seventeenth century, was challenged of course by Jean-Jacques Rousseau, who announces all the rhapsodies of the century to come. And Rousseau could be equally infuriating.

But Voltaire is eternally provoking. In the twentieth century his works were placed on the index of the Surrealist movement. In the nineteeth no one detested him more heartily than Baudelaire, momentartily deserted by his marvelous critical sense on the day he damned him as "the antipoet, the king of the boobies, the prince of the superficial, the antiartist, and the preacher fit for your concierge." Baudelaire forgot that Voltaire was an impeccable lawyer, and that a poet may need a lawyer.

Diderot simplified matters by claiming that "if Christ actually existed, I can tell you that Voltaire will be saved." Chateaubriand rendered a more profound judgment, even though he figured that Voltaire did not amount to much, having changed his mind too frequently on morals, philosophy, and religion. "He will charm you one day and bore you the next," Chateaubriand reported. "He would have been a madman if he had not been so wise, and would have been a wicked man if he had not been so often so decent. For all his impieties, he loathed the sophists. He had nothing in common with Diderot. . . . He was so elegant, his manners were so beautiful, and his benevolence ran so deep that very likely he would have ended as one of the great opponents of the Revolution. He was ever the champion of an orderly society, never comprehending that he was undermining its foundations by attacking religion."

Flaubert was more emphatic. "For me Voltaire is a *saint!*" he wrote. "Why do we have to call him a humbug because he was a fanatic? Does anyone obtain the results he got if one is not sincere? . . . I love him all the more when I think of those disgusting Voltaireans, the people who laugh at great ideals. Did *he* laugh? He ground his teeth."

Victor Hugo was generous when he came to salute the hundredth anniversary of Voltaire's death. "Voltaire won," said Hugo. "He defeated the legal system and all the old dogmas. He defeated the feudal lords, and Gothic judges, and the Roman priests. He elevated what had been the mob to the dignity of being the people. His smile put an end to violence, his sarcasm put an end to despotism, his irony put an end to infallibility, his perseverance put an end to stubbornness, and the truth he proclaimed put an end to ignorance.

"I've just pronounced the word *smile*," Hugo added. "And I must stop. The smile is Voltaire."

Voltaire was an accurate man, never so ruthless as when it came to eliminating the last trace of dust from his copy. No one could have read him more carefully than Heinrich von Kleist, whose Voltairean prose is one of the miracles of German literature. Voltaire deserved to become the most successful writer of the eighteenth century, rejoicing not only in the applause that pursued him but also in the money he so shrewdly invested. That he was not more bitterly hated for his success is a wonder, a wonder accounted for by his charm or by his apparent lack of conceit.

That he will ever be overlooked is inconceivable. His irreverence will save him. "Nothing is more disagreeable," he maintained, "than being hanged in some obsure place."

However, he has been dead for over two hundred years and possibly should not intrude too long on the twentieth century. This is a short book. He approved of short books. "The secret of being a bore," he said, "is to tell everything."

1

YOU MAY SAY THAT
I AM JEALOUS

Voltaire was a celebrity. In other words he was an actor, commanding with alarming confidence the stage of Europe from his château at Ferney outside the gates of Geneva. How to deal with this actor was a problem to many who sought out the great man on their Grand Tour, but not to the Prince de Ligne. At ease in the vast gardens of his Beloeil near Brussels, he made himself equally at home at Ferney. "The wise thing for me to do," he decided, "was never to let on how bright I was. I talked only to get him talking." So he began by asking: "I've heard there are a few authors you take seriously." "Yes," came the answer. "D'Alembert, for instance, who pretends to be a geometrician because he has no imagination. Then there is Diderot, who thinks he has some imagination. There's a pompous orator for you. They may say that I'm jealous. You must make up your own mind about that."

Oliver Goldsmith was easier to impress. "As a companion no man ever exceeded him when he pleased to lead the conversation, which, however, was not always the case. In company which he either disliked or despised, few could be more reserved than he; but when he was warmed in discourse, and had got over a hesitating manner which sometimes he was subject to, it was rapture to hear him."

Boswell, who did not forget to inform us that he himself was dressed in sea green and velvet on the day he paid his respects, was

6

taken not only with Voltaire but also with Father Adam, the unemployed Jesuit hired to let him win at chess. "I pray for Monsieur de Voltaire every day," said Father Adam. "Perhaps it will please God to touch his heart and make him see the true religion. It is a pity that he is not a Christian. He has many Christian virtues. He has the most beautiful soul."

This last thought did not occur to Gibbon, who failed to appreciate Voltaire's kindness in condescending to perform in one of his own plays before the guests. "Perhaps," Gibbon recalled, "I was too much struck with the ridiculous figure of Voltaire at seventy acting a Tartar conqueror with a hollow broken voice and making love to a very ugly niece of about fifty."

As for John Wilkes, who had been causing all the trouble he could for the British government, he found Voltaire "obliging beyond all expression." The Duchess of Northumberland would not have disagreed. Spellbound, she forgot his scrawny complexion, noting that he was "tall and rather genteel and has a fire in his eyes I never saw in those of a man of twenty-five. He had on a small well-combed dark grizzle tie-wig without powder, a lilac ribbon . . . around his neck, a pair of mignonette ruffles with a narrow edging, a long . . . waistcoat of brown satin with colored flowers, red velvet breeches, white worsted stockings and chamois shoes." When some one said in her presence: "If you subtract pride from priests, there is nothing left," Voltaire was equal to the occasion. "You don't think overeating counts for anything?" he asked.

As a rule Voltaire was at his best welcoming English and Americans. "By God, I do love the English, God dammit, if I don't love them better than the French, by God," he proclaimed in his best English in the spring of 1765. Which is enough to make us believe that Ralph Izard of Charleston arrived on a busy afternoon with his companion Arthur Lee of Virginia. "We were admitted no farther than his courtyard," Izard wrote home, "and upon sending in our names, the servant brought this answer: *Par dieu je suis malade.* We were taught to expect this before we went. His age and infirmities made him peevish, and the intrusion of many stupid young traveling Englishmen, who have visited him, as strangers do lions, in the tower, has given him such a disinclination to company that it is very difficult to get admittance to him." Unless, that is, he hoped that a visitor from the New World would be ready to join his anticlerical conspiracy. He was benevolent on presenting young Francis Kinloch of South Carolina to his circle. "You see a man," he announced, "who comes from the land of the savages but does not show it."

"No matter what you write," Voltaire was advised in his youth, "you will never succeed in destroying the Christian religion." "We shall see about that," he replied. Too much cannot be made of his contempt for Christianity. And since his obsession was not triggered by any one incident, he cannot be dismissed as a monomaniac. He was simply a man with a conviction that could not be erased.

He must have read and pondered Bossuet's funeral oration for Louis XIV's queen, Maria Theresa of Austria. "A Christian," Bossuet pointed out in this eulogy, "cannot be said to live on this earth, because he is perpetually mortified, and this mortification is a trial, an apprenticeship, a commencement of death." This is a beautiful argument, but made no impression on Voltaire, even though he led a never-ending crusade against atheism. The time has come to begin at the beginning.

Was Voltaire a bastard? This is doubtful, even if he hinted at this possibility in a bit of verse. François-Marie Arouet (he did not adopt the pseudonym of Voltaire, for no one knows what reason, until 1718) was born in Paris on November 21, 1694, the fifth and last child of the notary François Arouet and his wife Marie-Marguerite Daumart. Two older brothers died young. A sister, of whom he was quite fond, died when he was thirty-one, after marrying the civil servant Pierre-François Mignot and giving birth to two daughters, the elder of whom, the future Madame Denis, was to be Voltaire's companion and housekeeper for the last twenty-three years of his life. There remains the other brother, Armand, whom he cordially disliked—a serious-minded Jansenist who seems to have read enough of the theology of Port-Royal to become insufferable. (Jansenists might be described as Methodists masquerading as Romans.) "I have two crazy sons," said old Arouet. "One is crazy about religion, the other crazy against religion."

Voltaire's mother came from the minor nobility of Poitou. Voltaire's father's family had been tanners for generations. He himself was reasonably prosperous, numbering as he did the Duc de Saint-Simon among his clients, but was never guilty of encouraging his son at any time. Old Arouet could remember Corneille—"as boring a man as ever I met"—and thought that a writer was a creature "who wanted to be useless to society, a burden to his parents, and die of starvation." Saint-Simon, who could tolerate a poet or two when he was not wandering in the forest of family trees, conceded that Voltaire became a great poet, a man of standing in the republic of letters, and even an important person in a certain society he did not take the trouble to define.

His mother having died when he was seven, Voltaire was dispatched at ten to the *collège* of Louis-le-Grand, an excellent Jesuit school where he sincerely admired the teaching he received. "For seven years," he admitted, "I was educated by men who took no end of trouble to form the minds and watch over the morals of the younger generation. Why shouldn't one be grateful for teachers like those?" There was, however, a limit to his gratitude. "You wretch!" Father Le Jay one day answered his impertinence in the classroom. "The day is coming when you'll be the standard-bearer of deism in France."

"We were such big boys," recalled his schoolmate the Marquis d'Argenson, "and we were so wordly, that without being freethinkers, we were in a fair way to become such." Voltaire needed no encouragement in that direction. "I am tired," he said, "of hearing people say that only twelve men were needed to establish Christianity, and I'd like to prove that only one man is called for to undermine its foundations." In a more amiable mood he noted that in spite of all the fancy proofs advanced for the existence of God, no one had begun by talking of earthly joys. "Physically speaking," he argued, "pleasure is divine. And I believe that anyone who downs a glass of good Tokay wine or kisses a pretty woman or just feels good all over must recognize an omnipotent and considerate being."

He was not half so amiable on the day the now forgotten poet Jean-Baptiste Rousseau turned up at Louis-le-Grand to award him a prize for a poem he had just written. "He had a bad face," Rousseau reported, "but was wide awake and embraced me gracefully." Not too gracefully. "He should have confessed," Voltaire wrote later on, "that he paid this visit to the school because his father made my father's shoes, and my father got him a job in a lawyer's office. It is a shame he couldn't stay there, but he was sent away for lying about his family." The two were never to become too friendly. When Rousseau wrote an ode to posterity, Voltaire pointed out that "it will never reach the address." He must have been sincere at twenty-five when he advised Rousseau that the world was waiting for a new edition of his works "with the impatience they deserve."

The good priests of Louis-le-Grand were not the only ones to look after his education. His godfather, the Abbé de Châteauneuf, was so thoughtful as to introduce him when only eleven to the famous Ninon de L'Enclos, a woman of eighty whose first lover had been Cardinal Richelieu. When it was proposed in her old age that she enter a convent for repentant virgins, she declined on the grounds that she was neither repentant nor a virgin. She was suspected of saying only one prayer in her life: *Oh, Lord, make a man of the right sort—but never a woman of the right sort.* She may have been impressed by the verses Voltaire had begun to scribble, for she left him two thousand francs to buy books for his library.

The Abbé's brother, the Marquis de Châteauneuf, when appointed ambassador to the Hague, took Voltaire along as his page. He was then nineteen and old enough to fall in love. This he did, but the notion that he was ever desperately in love must be discarded. "Friendship," he declared long afterward, "is a thousand times more important to me than love. It seems quite evident to me that I am not a passionate man. In fact, there is something ridiculous in the idea of my ever falling in love." He seems to have recognized at an early age that the unhappy man is the man who is wasting his time.

One of his amusements at the Hague was Olympe Dunoyer, the daughter of a Protestant refugee. They should run off together, he planned, and he sent her boy's clothes in which to make her escape. "I don't know whether I should call you Mr. or

Miss," he was writing his "Pimpette," "but you are adorable, and our janitor, who is not in love with you, thought you were a very pretty boy." The plot was discovered, Châteauneuf was notified and incensed, and Voltaire sent back to Paris and his father. This was most unfortunate. Her lover had already decided that she should announce her conversion to the Roman Catholic faith: that would make her return to France so much easier.

He must study law, he was told by his father, and for a short time was a clerk. This was not the world in which he desired to move. The death of Louis XIV on September 1, 1715, and the assumption of the Regency by the Duc d'Orléans, the son of the king's bisexual brother, led to a relaxation of strict standards. This Voltaire was bound to approve, and he could not be too hard on Orléans: it was common knowledge that he whiled away the tedium of church at Christmastime by dipping into the volume of Rabelais he was careful to keep secret in his pew.

Encouraged, Voltaire saw no reason to hold his tongue. He could and did express himself on almost any subject with the libertines of the Temple, the group that gathered to salute the wit of the Grand Prieur de Vendôme on his return from exile. Voltaire himself was to know the meaning of exile. On the Regent's orders—he was supposed, rightly or wrongly, to be the author of some impertinent verses—he was ordered to take himself to Tulle, a good three hundred miles from Paris. However, the Regent relented and allowed him to approach two hundred miles nearer the capital, to Sully, the Gothic residence of the great-grandson of Henri IV's minister. "At Sully," he proclaimed, "I am a thousand times happier than the great prince who sent me into exile." This banishment did not last too long, and once he was free, Voltaire was welcomed at the best of châteaux. He was well acquainted with the interior of François Mansart's masterpiece, Maisons, made his way to Vaux, Fouquet's splendid seat, where the Maréchal de Villars, one of the great generals of Louis XIV, was spending his last years; and also enjoyed himself at Sceaux, just outside of Paris, where the Duchesse du Maine, the great-great-granddaughter of the Great Condé, held court in what had once been Colbert's domain. With her husband, Louis XIV's bastard by Madame de Montespan, she was busily plotting against the Regent, but not

so busily that she failed to charm her guest. "All those unfortunate princesses confined in enchanted castles by necromancers,"
he wrote her, "were unfailingly kind to wandering knights."

There were also anxious moments. "Monsieur Arouet," the
Regent greeted him one day, "I bet I can show you something you
haven't seen." "What is that?" "The Bastille!" came the answer.
From the sixteenth of May 1717 to the first of April 1718 he was
removed from circulation. He was allowed his Homer, his nightcap and two calico handkerchiefs, but his resentment could not be
concealed. "Do you know what that bugger did to me?" he
complained. "He sent me out of town for telling the public that
his Messalina of a daughter was no better than a whore." What
displeased the Regent was a Latin poem, "Puero Regnante," in
which he was accused, possibly accurately, of committing incest.
The Regent might not have been sure Voltaire was the author if
he had not bragged about "Puero Regnante" in the presence of a
spy by the name of Beauregard, who not only denounced him but
beat him up. Voltaire did not rest until Beauregard himself was
behind the bars.

Voltaire was irrepressible. "We are all princes here, or all
poets," he announced in the salon of the Prince de Conti. And he
presumed to dedicate his first play, *Oedipe*, having tried it on the
ears of Madame du Maine, to the Regent himself. (In the end it
was inscribed to the Regent's mother.) "Poor Voltaire," he teased
the Regent, "owes you much more than the privilege of having
spent a year in the Bastille. He was hoping that after shipping
him off to purgatory, you might remember him on the day you
open the gates of paradise to everyone."

Although the considerable twentieth-century scholar Daniel
Mornet decided that Voltaire's plays are no more entertaining
than schoolboy exercises, *Oedipe* may still be read without pain.
It was a hit on its opening night, November 17, 1718, and enjoyed
thirty consecutive performances. And even if there is no trace of
the customary grandeur of Corneille, it is far superior to the dreary
horrors of Crébillon's *Atrée et Thyeste*, which made its mark in
the previous decade.

Oedipe is more than a retelling of Sophocles: it may be the first
important anticlerical statement of the century. "I've forced the

gods to blush who forced me to commit my crimes," cries Jocaste at the end. She detests all priests with the fervor that Voltaire found so congenial.

> *Nos prêtres ne sont pas ce qu'un vain peuple pense,*
> *Notre crédulité fait toute leur science . . .*
>
> [*Our priests are not what weak people believe/Our credulity has given them all their wisdom . . .*]

Voltaire may have been charmed by his success at twenty-four, but was shrewd enough to realize that cash on hand may be the best companion that an author could ask for. "I've seen so many authors poor and despised," he emphasized, "that I decided a long time ago that I wasn't going to add to their number. In France one must be either an anvil or a hammer. I was born an anvil." He became the confidant of the Pâris brothers, financiers who steered clear of the chaos wrought by the Scotsman John Law. "I owe to you," he confessed to the Pâris brothers, "the fact that things have gone well with me. I shall never forget this."

On the subject of John Law Voltaire was explicit. "Has everyone gone insane in Paris?" he was writing in the summer of 1719. "Has half the country discovered the philosopher's stone in paper mills? And is Law a god, a crook, or a charlatan who has been poisoning himself with the drug he has been handing out to everyone? As for me, I can dream of nothing but poetry."

Not quite. Although Voltaire inherited an income of only £4,250 on his father's death in 1722, he knew how to increase his capital. "When I see Christians cursing Jews, methinks I see children beating their fathers," he observed. On one day he would sink a vast sum in a government lottery, positive that the big buyers would come out on top. On another he would gamble on the wheat trade with the Barbary Coast. On still another he would speculate in army contracts. On his deathbed he was enjoying an income of £231,000, which signified that he was one of the wealthiest citizens of France.

He was seldom careless in investing money but was not too particular in choosing who might help him puff his literary reputation. In 1725 he was so foolish as to befriend the Abbé

Pierre-François-Guyot Desfontaines, a hack writer sent to prison for corrupting young boys. "I can assure you he's incapable of the crime of which he is accused," Voltaire pleaded, and the Abbé was released. "I shall never forget all that I owe you," he promised. He did forget, and by 1738 issued the *Voltairomanie*, a libelous attack that was a delight to all Voltaire's enemies.

All this while Voltaire was mixing deism with love. One flagrant example of this was his affair with the Marquise de Ruplemonde, daughter of the Maréchal d'Alègre, with whom he set off in the summer of 1722 for Brussels and the Hague. In her honor he wrote the *Epître à Uranie*, described by an unqualified admirer as "a total condemnation of Christianity." It is not totally satisfactory as a poem.

The Voltaire that is easier to remember is the man who could usually forgive and forget the misdeeds of the great. He could joke, for instance, with the Regent the morning after the Bastille. "My Lord," he told him in a private audience, "I shouldn't object if Your Majesty deigned to provide my board, but I beg Your Highness to look after my lodging no longer."

But Voltaire had no intention of overlooking the indecency of the Chevalier Gui-Auguste de Rohan-Chabot, even though he happened to be the nephew of Anne de Rohan-Chabot, Princess de Soubise, for whom Pierre-Alexis Delamair designed the Hôtel de Soubise, one of the commanding townhouses of Paris. The quarrel began at the opera, where the Chevalier insulted him for taking a pseudonym. The quarrel was continued a couple of days later in the theater, where the Chevalier repeated his insults, this time in the presence of Adrienne Lecouvreur, an actress whose talent Voltaire respected. She fainted on hearing that a beating was promised.

Not long thereafter Voltaire was dining in the townhouse of the Duc de Sully when he was again interrupted by the Chevalier's crying out: "Who is that young man who talks so loud?" "Monsieur le Chevalier," someone answered, "he doesn't bear a great name, but he is an honor to the name he bears." Rohan-Chabot no sooner left the room than the guests broke into applause. "We are delighted," they told Voltaire, "that you have freed us from his presence." So runs one version of the incident. According to another, Rohan-Chabot was told: "I am the first of my name and you are the last of yours."

A few days later Voltaire was again dining with Sully when a servant came with the message that he was wanted. At the door were two men who asked him to come up to a carriage. Carrying out their orders, they beat him up while Rohan-Chabot sat watching. "Enough!" he finally announced. "Don't hit him on the head. Something good may come out of it in the end."

So Voltaire began practicing fencing to give Rohan-Chabot the punishment he deserved. Whether he was serious could be questioned. "Physical courage is one thing, mental courage another," commented his unfriendly friend the Marquis d'Argenson. "They are rarely met with in the same person. Voltaire may serve as an example. He is as brave as Turenne, Moses, or Gustavus Adolphus. But he is deathly afraid of injury and is a confirmed coward." The Bishop of Blois was equally unkind. "We'd be in quite a fix," he said, "if poets had no shoulders."

On April 17, 1726, came the inevitable *lettre de cachet*, expedited by the Chevalier's relative the Cardinal de Rohan. Voltaire was not released from the Bastille until the twenty-ninth, and after agreeing to take himself to England.

This was not a forbidding destination. *Londres, jadis barbare, est le centre des arts,* he declared in the first canto of *La Henriade,* the epic poem on Henri IV he had published in England in 1723. This found him at least one attentive reader across the channel. "I conclude him," wrote Pope to his friend Viscount Bolingbroke, "at once a freethinker and a lover of quiet; no bigot, yet no heretic, one who honors national sanctions without prejudice to truth and charity."

It is true that Pope wished for more of the fictitious in this epic. And it is also true that the twentieth-century critic Daniel Mornet was able once again to restrain his admiration. "What isn't stolen from Virgil, is stolen from Lucan, Tasso or Ariosto. It is written by everyone except Voltaire," he declared. Perhaps the kindest thing that could be said of *La Henriade* is that it was the work of an historian posing as a poet.

The kindest thing that could be said of Voltaire himself is that he could occasionally let bygones be bygones. "I can forgive you for having gone to the opera with the Chevalier de Rohan," he wrote from London in the fall of 1726 to his dear friend the Marquise de Bernières, "provided you felt a trifle embarrassed about it. Most women are either passionate or indolent, but I think I know you well enough to hope for your friendship. If you are a friend of mine, you must write me from time to time."

2

POETRY IS NO LONGER
THE FASHION AT PARIS

Voltaire was a talented journalist. By this no insult is intended. He was no superficial explorer of England. He might be biased but could think on his feet and proved it the second he reached London and began to master the English language.

"There was not a cloud in the sky," he bravely reported. This was not quite true. Even though the Aleppo merchant Everard Fawkener put him up at his home in Wandsworth, two bankers holding Voltaire's letters of credit went immediately into bankruptcy. He was, however, recognized as a gentleman of importance: Louis XV's foreign minister had recommended him to the French ambassador, besides asking the British ambassador in Paris to say a word in his favor to the Duke of Newcastle. Moreover, he was well acquainted with Henry Saint John, Viscount Bolingbroke, who knew everyone worth knowing, no matter if the intrigues in which he entered with his one-time associate Robert Harley, Earl of Oxford, led in the end to disgrace and even exile. "What a world is this," cried Bolingbroke on the death of Queen Anne, "and how has Fortune bantered us!"

Bolingbroke, who held that "the landed men are the true owners of our political vessel; the moneyed men, as such, are no more than passengers on it," could not share Voltaire's reverence for crisp bills. In the end Voltaire found him prolix, despite his battle against prejudice. But he had taken a French wife, and his command of French was unmistakable. He had, Voltaire declared, "all the learning of his country and all the politeness of ours. This man, who has been devoted all his life to pleasure and business, has found time for learning everything and retaining everything."

One of Bolingbroke's intimate friends was Alexander Pope, whom Voltaire would one day describe as "a wretch whose impious pen dares brag of God's infinite mercy." But we are moving ahead of our story. Pope had not yet written *An Essay on Man*— dedicated to Bolingbroke—when he and Voltaire first met, and no one could tell that he would be guilty of asserting that "whatever IS, is RIGHT."

In the *Philosophical Letters* recording his sojourn in England Voltaire made plain that Pope was the most elegant, correct, and harmonious poet the nation had yet produced: "He has trained the harsh whistle of the English trumpet to imitate the sweet sounds of the flute." Voltaire also allowed that Pope and his rivals had learned much from the French. "In our turn we should borrow from them. . . . We and the English followed after the Italians, who were our masters in every respect, and whom we have now and then surpassed. I can't say which of the three countries deserves the preference, but lucky is the man who can appreciate all three."

As for what went on when he called on Pope at Twickenham we are still in the dark. According to one story he showed up before learning English. This visit was not a success. On another occasion he is said to have so offended Pope's mother by his coarse language that she left the room. This may or may not have been true. The most often quoted account of the incident is third hand, transmitted by Thomas Gray, who had no use for Voltaire whatever. He must have a very good stomach, Gray believed, who can digest his warmed-over cabbage: "Atheism is a vile dish, though all the cooks of France combine to make a new sauce for it." He was unaware that Voltaire was no atheist and made the further mistake of attributing to him a trip to Italy.

For Voltaire in the fall of 1726 Pope was the best poet "at present of all the world. It may be," he told a French friend, "French folly is pleasanter than English madness, but by God,

19

English wisdom and English honesty is above yours." He was
equally eloquent on the subject of Swift, whom he seems to have
met at Twickenham. "The more I read your works, the more
ashamed I am of mine," he declared. Perhaps, then, he should be
forgiven for passing him off as the Rabelais of England. He did
admit that Rabelais was a drunk philosopher who only wrote
when drunk. This could hardly be said of the Dean of Saint
Patrick's. He loathed Lent, which was in his favor; he also resented
the "sour, devout faces of people who only put on religion for
seven weeks." The difficulty was that his sense of humor was
occasionally a match for Voltaire's own. A prize example of this
was his argument against abolishing Christianity in England.

Although bewildered by the glory of Sir John Vanbrugh's
designs for Blenheim Palace, Voltaire could enjoy his comedies as
easily as those of Congreve or Wycherley. Shakespeare presented a
different problem. Prisoner that he was of the rules of rhetoric of
seventeenth-century France, rhetoric that he put to excellent account in his own prose, Voltaire was embarrassed by the liberties
that Shakespeare could not help taking. "His real accomplishment," he pointed out, "was a catastrophe for English drama.
There are such beautiful scenes, such great and frightening fragments in his monstrous farces that they call tragedies, that his
plays have always been performed with great success. Time, which
settles all reputations, has rendered all their errors respectable."
The gravediggers in *Hamlet,* for instance, were inexcusable. No
such mistake could be found in Addison's *Cato.*

Shakespeare was to worry Voltaire all his life. As late as 1776 he
was lamenting the fact that "this monster has his admirers in
France, and to compound this horror, I was the first Frenchman
to mention his name. I was the first to reveal a few pearls I had
discovered in his enormous manure pile."

He must have his say on the subject of Pascal as well, even
though we may wonder why he was included in this English
miscellany. Although he died thirty-two years before Voltaire was
born, he would not vanish from the horizon. He was resented as
no one else. Nor could his wit be slighted. As a Jansenist he had
joyfully exposed the fallacies of Jesuitical reasoning in the *Lettres
Provinciales.* Respect was called for. Yet he was a Christian,

bearing consolation to the tormented. In Voltaire's eyes the tormented or troubled were not only foolish, they were unnecessary. Uncommon sense should solve all difficulties. The cry of Pascal's Christ: "You would not have sought me if you had not already found me"—was ridiculous.

So Voltaire began belaboring Pascal. "I dare," he wrote, "to take the side of humanity against this sublime misanthropist. I dare to assert that we are neither so wicked nor so miserable as he claims."

Pascal was given to examining both the grandeur and the misery of mankind. This was a waste of time. Christianity teaches merely simplicity, humanity, and charity; wandering off into metaphysics can lead only to one error after another. As for Pascal's argument that failing to bet on the existence of God is the equivalent of betting that He does not exist, this was the sort of logic that could turn us all into atheists. And Pascal was slow witted when he listed the weak points of Montaigne, among them his approval of suicide. Montaigne, Voltaire proved to his own satisfaction, was talking as a philosopher, not as a Christian. Worst of all, he hinted, was Pascal's insistence that if God exists, we must love only Him and not our fellow creatures. This command might fascinate Nietzsche, but not Voltaire.

In his old age Voltaire was to dwell again on this obsession with Pascal. He was a great writer, he conceded, but hardly a great man. And his reverence for the Jews was incomprehensible. What was God's chosen people but a band of thieves and usurers, superstitious and bloody-minded. Humanity could be a closed corporation.

Eighteenth-century London was a more congenial subject. If there were only one faith in England, despotism would be a constant threat. If there were two, the English would soon be cutting their own throats. But there were thirty different varieties, and the result was the English lived in peace with each other. That this peace might be due to indifference or even apathy did not concern Voltaire.

The trust in reason of this deist was not only immoderate, it was irrational, which made him the most prominent representative of the Enlightenment, the conspiracy hatched to prove that all man's troubles on earth would vanish once the rule of reason was acknowledged. This conspiracy did bring certain blessings to mankind, including Thomas Jefferson's Declaration of Independence, based in part on John Locke's championship of Natural Rights. That these Natural Rights could never be perfectly defined did not embarrass either Locke, Jefferson, or Voltaire.

Voltaire was enchanted by Locke's dismissal of the doctrine of innate ideas. Once this doctrine was dethroned, we might leap any number of hurdles and so establish a rational universe superintended by a rational God who had nothing whatever in common with the Christian sects. "Let us suppose," Locke had said, "the mind to be, as we say, white paper void of all characters, without any ideas. How comes it to be so furnished? To this I answer, from EXPERIENCE. In all that our knowledge is founded." And when Locke went on to insist that "there is no error to be named which has not its professors," Voltaire could only rejoice. He did not need to be reminded of the errors of Christianity.

Locke was to question whether a purely material being was or was not capable of thinking. There were theologians who cried that he aimed to overturn religion. Not at all, said Voltaire. This was a merely philosophical question, and philosophers would never harm the religion established in any country. "Why? Because philosophers are never guilty of enthusiasm, and besides they are not writing for the common people."

Locke was one hero. Another was Sir Isaac Newton, whose funeral Voltaire had the honor of attending in 1727. Newton was not exactly unknown in France, having been made an *associé étranger* of their Academy of Sciences in 1699. This was something, but it was not enough. It became Voltaire's ambition to undermine the reputation of Descartes and to substitute the cult of Newton in its stead. There was no denying that Descartes had made geometry perform miracles, but then he had become the slave of his own system, and his "philosophy" was no better than an ingenious novel. He was, Voltaire decided, wrong about the nature of the soul, wrong when it came to proving the existence of God, wrong about the laws of motion, and wrong about the nature of light. Worse yet, he admitted the existence of innate ideas.

And Newton? He was the master of the laws of gravitation and motion, the perfect guide for students of the geometry of the infinite. Mankind should be grateful for his reflecting telescope and for his investigation of the properties of light.

While pondering these things Voltaire was not the man to neglect his own interests. There was the question of distributing *La Henriade* in England. George II had been so thoughtful as to send him twenty guineas when his letters of credit became worthless. What could be more appropriate than dedicating this poem to the queen, Caroline of Anspach? She was a redoubtable bluestocking but did approve of deists, provided she could talk about her passion, which was theology. "Our learned Queen," Bolingbroke had written, "interests herself in nice and subtle disputations about space; from metaphysics she rises to theology. She attends frequently to the controversy, almost fourteen hundred years old and still carried on with much warmth and as little success, about that profound mystery, the Trinity."

Subscribers to *La Henriade* were called for, and Voltaire got them. Sir Robert Walpole was helpful. So was Lord Chesterfield, who signed for ten copies. Dining at Chesterfield's was delightful; the only vexation was having to tip the lord's staff. Moving farther and farther into the great world, he braved even the Duchess of Marlborough. Her first impression of him was favorable, even though she took him at thirty-four to be at least sixty. "Here is a Frenchman," she remarked, "that I believe is about threescore, who has learned in a year's time to read all the English authors and both to write and speak English." But when he asked for a look at her memoirs, she hesitated. "Wait a little," she advised him. "I am at present altering my account of Queen Anne's character. I have begun to love her again since the present lot have become our governors." In the end she had her misgivings, perhaps because he found the language of her memoirs too vitriolic. "I thought the man had sense, but I find him at bottom either a fool or a philosopher."

"What a girl you are!" Pope dared write the duchess when she failed to keep an appointment. Pope's independent spirit was admirable, and Voltaire was ready to believe that merit was recognized in England: Addison had been made a secretary of state, Swift a dean in Ireland, and Newton was buried in Westminster Abbey. However, Voltaire was saddened when he recalled that when it came to patronizing the arts no one was so magnificent as Louis XIV. It was time to return to France. He had received official permission for a three-day trip in the summer of 1727 and may have made another stealthy excursion. On the fifteenth of March 1729 he did obtain the right to go home, settling first in Saint-Germain-en-Laye and then in Paris.

In Paris on March 15, 1730, he was watching the performance of Adrienne Lecouvreur as Jocaste in *Oedipe*. Her declamation was so natural that she worked a real revolution in the French theater. But this was her last appearance. She died a few days later in Voltaire's arms while her latest lover, the Maréchal de Saxe, was looking on. The curé of Saint-Sulpice, Jean-Baptiste-Joseph Languet de Gergy, was sent for. The brother of the Bishop of Châlons, who made a sensation popularizing the raptures of Marguerite-Marie Alacoque of the Order of the Visitation, Languet was an excellent administrator, raising the money for Servandoni's portal to the church and founding the Hospital of the enfant-Jésus for destitute girls. He may have deserved his splendid tomb at Saint-Sulpice by Michel-Ange Slodtz. Yet he chose to be officious when Adrienne lay dying and demanded an act of repentance for the scandals of her profession, this and the solemn renunciation of the theater the Church required before granting the final sacraments. These conditions could hardly be met in the presence of Voltaire. So she was denied Christian burial, and her corpse tossed into a pile of quicklime on the banks of the Seine. Furious, Voltaire recalled that the body of the English actress Anne Oldfield was laid to rest in Westminster Abbey. An infamous insult had been offered Adrienne by cruel priests, he claimed in his elegy for the incarnation of Jocaste:

> Que direz-vous, race future
> Lorsque vous apprendrez la flétrissante injure
> Qu'à ces arts désolés font des prêtres cruels.

[*What will you say, men of the future,/When you learn of the degrading insult/The cruel priests are offering these disconsolate arts.*]

As a deist Voltaire could hardly take seriously the comfortable words of the Christian religion. This was obvious on January 27,

1733, when he had the privilege of observing the last moments of the Baronne de Fontaine-Martel, with whom he was living at the time. All night long he was watching over this mistress; all day long he was taking care of her house. "Just imagine," he wrote a friend, "I was the one who had to tell the poor woman that the time had come to say good-bye. She didn't want anything to do with the last ceremonies, but I was bound to see to it that she died according to the regulations. I brought her a priest, half a Jansenist and half a politician, who made a pretense of giving her confession and then came to give her everything else on the bill. When this comedian from Saint-Eustache asked if she weren't convinced that her God, her creator, was in the eucharist, she answered *Oh, yes!* in a way that would have made me break out laughing in less lugubrious circumstances. I did all I could to induce the dying woman to leave something to her servants and especially to a young woman of good family that she had recently taken on and torn away from her family in the hope she had given her of remembering her in her will. But the Baronne was inflexible, and didn't want to give anyone in the house any reason to regret her. Three years before this she had written a will disinheriting her only daughter as much as she could. But since this time she had done her house over and also her friends. Right now I have all the trouble of finding a new place to live in and of rescuing my furniture which got mixed up with that of the Baronne. Without all this trouble that descended upon me, my new tragedy would be almost finished." The Baronne de Fontaine-Martel could not have been too distressed by all this. When she began to fail, she asked what time it was. "Two o'clock," she was told. "God be praised," she murmured, "no matter what time it is, there's always a boy meeting a girl someplace."

By now Voltaire had begun to suspect that his talents were not appreciated by the French government. On the tenth of June, 1734, *Philosophical Letters* was ordered burned "as scandalous, contrary to religion, good morals, and the respect due authority." It was true that he had not been too reverent in discussing the Church of England, that he had poked fun at the quaintness of the Quakers, and that he set Newton over Descartes. Above all, he suggested there was room for improvement in France. So the unfortunate publisher was sent to the Bastille and the warrant for the arrest of the author issued as early as the eighth of May: he was to be escorted, on the king's orders, to the castle of Auxonne in Burgundy. He escaped, having skipped town, and his whereabouts were for the moment unknown.

Let no one believe that Voltaire was being persecuted by Louis XV. "The timid, yet vainglorious young man"—so he appeared to the Duc de Saint-Simon—who inherited the throne at the age of five in 1715, was no tyrant at heart. Overwhelmed by the prestige of his great-grandfather, Louis XIV, he seemed searching for the personality he would never acquire. There was even a time when it was thought he would never like girls. This taste had to be cultivated. Once implanted, it was permanent. Married at fifteen to Marie Leczinska, the devout twelve-year-old daughter of the exiled King Stanislas of Poland, he became the father of ten children in twelve years.

However, he rarely made use of what imagination he had. When a doe presumed to lick his hand, he shot her dead. He may have been merely careless at the moment. He certainly was not careless as a boy when he made a present of a watch to a page, burying it deep in a box full of mud so that he could quietly enjoy the scramble for the prize. He himself was never eager to fight for the prizes to be won by an aggressive foreign policy. As a child he watched with apparent approval the caution—or ineptitude—of the Duc de Bourbon, who manufactured an alliance with England and Holland. There was a war, but it was brief, with Spain, then ruled by his uncle, Philip V. The Regency came to an end with Orléans' death in 1723, but no adventures were in the offing. Once Bourbon was succeeded by Cardinal Fleury, the ally of Sir Robert Walpole in England, peace became the objective, peace and prosperity. In less than thirty years the foreign trade of France quadrupled.

Was this the only purpose of government? Voltaire was too ambitious to agree. "The French," he announced in the opening pages of his biography of Charles XII of Sweden, the first volume of which was issued in 1731, "are born to obey, win in battle, and cultivate the arts. Yet anyone who glanced at the memoirs of the early years of the reign of Louis XV would have to swear that we were indifferent to everything except the charms of indolence and greed."

Although Viscount Bolingbroke thought the *History of Charles XII* "the best piece of modern history that hath lately appeared in public," the French government thought differently. The book was immediately seized by the police on the grounds that the author had been indelicate in describing Charles XII's rival, Augustus Elector of Saxony and King of Poland (one of whose illegitimate children was Maurice de Saxe). The world was to fasten on this history, thanks only to surreptitious editions issuing from Basel, Amsterdam, and London. Here was the true beginning of Voltaire's never-ending quarrel with censorship.

For the first time Voltaire's historical mind was apparent. "After having read three or four thousand descriptions of battles," he complained, "I found I was no better off than before I began. I was only learning about events." He was concerned with more than events. He aimed to illuminate the worst vices or greatest virtues of a nation, why it was powerful or negligable at sea and to what degree it had grown richer in the last century. He would encompass the spread of trade and the rise of the arts as they affected one country and then another. He would also never neglect the changes that came about in laws and moral customs. In this way the history of mankind could be judged, not just the petty rivalries of kings and courts. Details could be tolerated, but only to prove points.

The *History of Charles XII* is more than the mere chronicle of the insane ambition of a king. "His passion for glory, war, and vengeance kept him from being a sure politician," Voltaire remarked. He was properly impressed by Charles's victory over Peter the Great at Narva in Esthonia in 1700; this did mean more than his quick conquest of Denmark in six weeks. But then he began his suicidal march into the Ukraine, ending in 1709 in the disaster at Pultava. Not that disaster could humiliate Charles. He was an outrageous prisoner. Equally outrageous was his return to Scandinavia, where he died at thirty-six besieging Frederickshall in Norway.

Voltaire's Charles XII is always comprehensible. So is Peter the Great for whom he had far more respect. So is Augustus II, whose court at Dresden he ranked second only to that of Louis XIV. And

Voltaire is tactful but not servile when he comes to Stanislas Leczinski, Charles's unfortunate candidate for Augustus's role as King of Poland, who would end his days as Louis XV's pensioner at Nancy in Lorraine.

Voltaire, who may or may not have suspected that the dust would never settle on the *History of Charles XII*, could never rid himself of his passion for the theater. In December 1730 he brought out *Brutus*, dedicated to Bolingbroke. Its receipts were never eloquent, it is just another one of the fifty-odd plays that are neither read nor performed in our century, but he was willing to believe that this might do as well at the box office as *Oedipe*. He wrote a charming letter to Marie-Ange Dangeville, the young girl cast as Tullie.

"I've had a bad night," he told her. "Otherwise I'd throw myself at your feet to thank you for the honor you are doing me today. The play is not worthy of you, but think of the glory that may be yours for gracing the role of Tullie. My success or failure depends on you. You must remember not to hurry, to brighten every line, and to sigh from time to time . . . Don't be discouraged, just think how marvelous you were in the rehearsals. Your timidity does you great honor. Tomorrow you must take your revenge . . . And even if everything doesn't go well, what of it? You are only fifteen years old, and all they can say is that you are not yet what you will become . . . Good-bye. It's up to you to be divine tomorrow."

The reception of *Zaïre*, produced in the summer of 1732, was as encouraging as that of *Brutus* had been depressing. Voltaire himself played the role of the fanatical Lusignan in this drama set in the time of the Crusades, and his obvious aim was to remind the world of the inadequacy of Christian morality: the Saracen Orosmane is the humane hero, killing himself when told that Lusignan is the father of Zaïre, the Christian slave he had hoped to marry. However, Orosmane has already killed Zaïre, caught escaping with her brother Nérestan. The plot is complicated, but then we must remember that Voltaire devoted only twenty-two days to this tragedy.

The preface, rather than the text, may be the arresting thing about *Zaïre* in the twentieth century. The play was dedicated to Voltaire's English friend Fawkener. He was a businessman, and businessmen, the argument runs, are entitled to far more respect than idlers, whether French or English. Besides, Louis XIV encouraged both Racine and the woolen manufacturer Van Robais. From here Voltaire goes on to prove that the ideal government is bound to encourage arts and letters. "The world is full of countries as powerful as we are," he argues. "And why do we look down on them? We despise them just as we do a rich man who has no education and no taste . . . There is nothing frivolous about the honor of serving as a model for other nations: the arts are a sure sign of grandeur."

Nor should the sciences be neglected. "Poetry is no longer the fashion at Paris," he was telling one of his friends in the spring of 1735. "Everyone I know is turning into a geometrician or a physicist. They are reasoning like mad. Sentiment, the imagination, and the graces have been sent into exile. A man who had lived under Louis XIV and came back to this world would no longer recognize the French. He might even believe that the Germans had conquered our country. The *belles lettres* have fallen into a visible decline."

Was this an accurate analysis of France in 1735? Or was Voltaire merely speaking his own mind? His sympathy for the arts was always more intellectual than real. He once thought of asking Oudry to turn out a few tapestries based on *La Henriade*, but gave up the idea when the price came too high. Nor is there any record of his rewarding Boucher, Fragonard, or Chardin. The most beautiful chairs the world will ever see were then being created by the French *ébénistes*, but he was not extravagant in this direction. So far as we know, his only interesting acquisition was a sofa and four armchairs by Avisse.

And music? For Voltaire Rameau was a pedant, precise and boring. He was simply a fool, he declared, a fool following the advice of connoisseurs who did not know their business. "That is why he has never composed a good opera and never will."

Moreover, when he talked of the decline of *belles lettres*, he chose to ignore the lovely, poetic comedies of Marivaux which have enchanted the twentieth century. He is silent, for instance, on *Les Jeux de l'Amour et du Hasard*, which saw the stage in the same year as *Brutus*. "I hope," he remarked, "that he will write one day in a less affected style and treat more noble subjects." He never did. Voltaire was also frightened at the thought that Marivaux might denounce him in print. He never did.

Poetry was decidedly not the fashion at Cirey, the château in Champagne of Emilie Le Tonnelier de Breteuil, Marquise du Châtelet. She believed in popularizing deism and the sciences, and she kept Voltaire from completing his manuscript on Louis XIV. But it was with her that he sought refuge in 1733, not long after he fled Paris because of the *Philosophical Letters*.

The most unfriendly portrait of the Marquise du Châtelet was the work of the Marquise du Deffand, the wisest woman Voltaire would ever know. "Just imagine," Madame du Deffand wrote, "a big dried-up woman with no hips, big arms, big legs, enormous feet, a very small head, a sharp face, a pointed nose, two little sea-green eyes, a dark complexion, a dull mouth, and teeth infrequent and decayed. There is beautiful Emilie for you, and she is so proud of her shape that she spares no expense to show it off. She will have her hair curled, she dotes on tassels, precious stones, and fine beads. Nothing is ever too much. But as she wants to be beautiful in spite of herself, and magnificent without spending much money, she often has to get along without stockings, chemises, handkerchiefs, and other trifles."

3

UNHAPPINESS IS
UNNECESSARY

Marie de Vichy, Marquise du Deffand, could not be extinguished. Although she went blind at fifty-five, her real vision was never impaired until the day she died at eighty-three. When recalling her friendship of fifty-odd years with one of the principal fixtures of her salon, she did not hesitate to tell him that the reason they had been friends for so long was that they meant nothing to each other. Nor did she shrink from revealing the truth as she saw it to the most entertaining man she knew, Horace Walpole, who kept seeking her company in Paris when away from Strawberry Hill, his Gothic castle at Twickenham. "You are magnificent when it comes to the *hors-d'oeuvre*," she told him. He never made the advances she would have enjoyed.

She was easily bored. This her husband realized. He was discarded when she was twenty-five. She also knew that religion was a tedious topic for conversation and refused to quarrel over it. "Leave those priests alone and all that stuff," she dared remind Voltaire when he wrote one sermon too many on the defects of Christianity. "Your task is to reaffirm good taste. Deliver us from fraudulent eloquence and lay down the principles. And since your example is not sufficient, you must assume the command of your empire and dismiss from your government the people who have turned into dictators, judging like so many sovereigns, good or evil, the problem of good and evil. These followers of yours know nothing of the world, nothing about decorum, nothing about deference, nothing about good breeding, nothing about the arts, including the art of getting on in the world, and nothing about morals. You have created these people. Now you must imitate Him in whom you believe, and do penance for what you have done."

To the eternal credit of Voltaire, this frank statement did no damage to their friendship.

To be accurate at all times was one of his aims. He also believed—a few of us may agree with this in our ruthless moments with ourselves—that unhappiness was unnecessary. Grief could be, if not erased, at least dismissed by paying meticulous attention to the problem of imposing oneself on one's century. So in the sixteen-odd years he spent with Emilie du Châtelet at Cirey he did his best to eliminate the threat of Montesquieu in the literary world, tried his hand at diplomacy, joined the French Academy, made a place for himself at the court of Louis XV, and welcomed the dubious advances of Frederick the Great.

Whether the "divine Emilie," who was twenty-seven when she and the thirty-nine-year-old Voltaire began living together, was an attractive woman is difficult to ascertain. She *may* have been more presentable than the Marquise du Deffand would have us believe. In any event there is no doubt that she was an industrious if not always cheerful intellectual. At fifteen she had begun her own translation of Virgil and by the time she joined Voltaire set her mind to mastering English in order to be a worthy companion. She was enchanted by Newton and irritated by the Bible. Her major effort—at least it has been attributed to her—was a 738-page study of the errors to be found in the Book of Genesis. This remains unpublished. She recognized, as she read the Bible, that the laws of physics were violated by the separation of light from darkness, and she went on to write an essay, which attracted some attention at the time, on the nature of fire. But her greatest accomplishment, in the opinion of one Voltaire scholar, was seeing to it that he completed his education on the subject of English deism. Unfortunately, and this may be held against her by those who enjoy the *Age of Louis XIV*, she believed that this work should be postponed indefinitely.

One of the charms of the château of Cirey was that the Marquis du Châtelet was rarely on hand. Cirey remains today a warm, friendly house, and even if it will never deserve mention in a history of French architecture, its stairway is inviting, and there was room for a tiny theater in which Voltaire could try out one after another of his never-ending list of dramas.

One drama to which Voltaire paid scant attention was the relationship between his Emilie and the Duc, later the Maréchal de Richelieu. The great-grandnephew of the cardinal, this Richelieu fancied not without reason that he was irresistible to all women and appears to have enjoyed Emilie before Voltaire came on the scene. The two parted without bitterness. She could write to him that "I'm in luck, because I can love in you the friend of my lover." He did grant Voltaire an annuity of £40,000. Besides, he was a man worth knowing. Although it would be farfetched to assume that he was the father of Louis XV, it is true that he was caught as a young man hiding under the bed of His Majesty's mother. Later on he would be a most intimate friend of the Duchesse de Châteauroux, the third of the famous Mailly sisters who shared Louis XV's bed.

It was wise of Voltaire and Emilie to turn up in the spring of 1734 for Richelieu's wedding to Elisabeth-Sophie de Lorraine, the daughter of the Prince de Guise. On this occasion he composed a poem for the bride and groom. "Don't love each other too much," he warned them. "That's the surest way to go on loving each other forever." Louis XV might have approved these sentiments, although he is known to have expressed certain misgivings about Richelieu's maneuvers. "If you chase him out of your front door, he'll be sure to come back down the chimney," he declared.

In the meantime Voltaire was pondering, with Emilie at his side, the existence or nonexistence of God and the problem of free will. The resulting *Treatise on Metaphysics,* summing up his conclusions, was not to be published until after his death. It does not make for alarming reading in the twentieth century, but we must suppose that Emilie treasured every word of this deistical argument.

Would a diet of deism oblige Voltaire to behave as he should? This was very much on Emilie's mind as she unburdened herself to Richelieu in the spring of 1735. "The longer I think about Voltaire's situation and my own, the more I am convinced that I'm doing what is right," she wrote. "First of all, I believe that people who are passionately in love would live together in the country if they could. But I also believe that only in the country may I hold his imagination in check. Sooner or later, I'd lose him in Paris, or at least I'd spend my days in fear of letting him slip away, and I know I'd have sufficient grounds to complain about him."

Voltaire's wings must be clipped, she decided: the mischievous man must be kept out of mischief at all cost. "I just can't comprehend," she went on to Richelieu, "how he can be so witty, so reasonable and everything else and be so blind about doing things that will ruin his reputation. But I must see what happens. I love him enough, I must tell you, to give up the joys of Paris for the happiness of leading a quiet life with him and the pleasure of saving him from his follies and his fate."

So it was no accident that Voltaire and Emilie spent only five weeks at the Hôtel Lambert, the townhouse she acquired as an investment in Paris real estate. Here was the luxury Voltaire claimed that he could not live without. For the Hôtel Lambert, designed by Louis LeVau, the very man who would later create the immense château of Vaux-le-Vicomte for Louis XIV's finance minister Fouquet, was gloriously decorated by LeBrun and Lesueur.

"I love luxury. I love to be indolent," Voltaire proclaimed in "Le Mondain," or "Man About Town," the short poem he published in 1736. Was he sincere in his ecstasy over living in the terrestrial paradise men call the present? This may be questioned. And we may never comprehend the dreadful anxiety that overcame him once this hymn to extravagance was put into print. For two months he hid in Holland under an assumed name before returning to the quiet of Cirey. Incidentally, this was the very year that, surrendering for once to a genuine artist, he had his pert portrait done by Maurice Quentin de la Tour.

All this while Emilie had no idea of giving up her friendship for Richelieu. "I must confess," she wrote him, "that if, after having forced me to count on your friendship, you stopped loving me, no, but stopped saying you loved me, if your interest in me abated to the slightest degree, if the conversation or the jokes of the people I am pleasing today and shall displease tomorrow made any difference to you, I'd be desperate. That's the way I am when it comes to friendship, and no matter how much I may distrust myself, my heart tells me that I must ask my friends to stand by me to the end. It seems to me that Voltaire is enjoying himself, and I am delighted."

He was not exactly happy, however, for he could not help noticing that Charles de Secondat, Baron de Montesquieu, was acquiring a certain reputation for the elegance of his prose. Montesquieu was also a sharp critic and proved it in his *Persian Letters*, where more than one malicious observation on French civilization could be discovered. "Can you conceive of a book in which our government and our religion are treated with less respect?" Voltaire complained in the summer of 1733. "Yet this book is responsible for the author's admittance into the band known as the French Academy." A year later he was displeased to find that Montesquieu had dared to write an essay on Roman history. "Have you seen the little, the too little book on the decadence of the Empire?" he asked. "They call it the decadence of Montesquieu." Most lamentable was Montesquieu's *L'Esprit des Lois*, his major work. He was well pleased to hear that Madame du Deffand referred to it as *De l'Esprit sur les Lois*, or *Witty Sayings about Laws*.

Montesquieu was disquieting. Equally disquieting was the presumption of Pierre-Louis Moreau de Maupertuis to pose as an authority on Isaac Newton. Here caution, for the time being, was called for. Maupertuis was an astronomer of some consequence and would soon set off for Lapland to measure the length of a degree on the meridian, so verifying Newton's thesis that the earth was an oblate spheroid, that is, a spheroid with flattened ends.

For the moment, reverence was advisable. Voltaire wrote Maupertuis that he had read his latest contribution seven or eight times over. "You are sublime; you are teaching me to think." Emilie joined in the chorus. She was, she said, more than grateful for his recent offerings. "I have," she admitted, "spent a whole evening profiting from your teachings." He may or may not have seduced her at this time. Scholars have hinted at an affair.

Voltaire was in need of praise as never before. It came from Berlin. On August 8, 1736, Frederick, Crown Prince of Prussia, wrote him as follows: "Dear Sir, Although I have not the satisfaction of knowing you personally, I am familiar with your works. They are veritable treasures of the mind. As for your poems, they are a course of instruction in morality, teaching men how to think and how to act. No one can imitate Voltaire unless it be Voltaire himself, and I have come to realize that being well born and dreaming of grandeur, all this amounts to nothing, or to tell the truth, nothing at all."

Although Voltaire would later remind Frederick in no uncertain terms that he would never master the French language, he found no fault with his prose when he replied on the first of September. "One would," he said, "have to be really insensitive not to be deeply touched by the letter with which Your Royal Highness has deigned to honor me. It was indeed flattering to my self-esteem, but the love of mankind, which I have always had in my heart, and which, I dare say, is the essence of my character, gave me a pleasure a thousand times more pure when I understood that there exists a prince who thinks like a man, a philosopher-prince intent on making men happy . . . The only good kings are those who have begun, as you have, to educate themselves, to know what men are like, to love the truth, and to detest persecution and superstition. A prince who thinks these thoughts may well bring back the golden age to his kingdom. I can see that the Newtons, the Leibnitzes, the Bayles, and the Lockes, those noble souls, so well informed and so benevolent, are the ones who have nourished your mind, and that you scorn as poisonous and trivial all other so-called intellectual food.

"I shall look upon it as a precious advantage to come to pay court to Your Royal Highness. People go to Rome to see the churches, the pictures, the ruins, and the bas-reliefs. A prince like you is far more deserving of such a voyage, but the friend who detains me in my present retreat will not allow me to leave."

Years later Voltaire would tell us that "Frederick's father gave him no share in the government and that there really was no government at all in his country, only one military review after another. So he spent his leisure writing to men of letters in France who were not exactly unknown. Most of the burden fell on me. He sent me poetical letters, he sent me treatises on metaphysics, history, and politics. He treated me as though I were divine. I treated him as though he were Solomon. All these epithets did not cost anything. They have printed some of this nonsense in my complete works, and fortunately they have printed only one thirtieth." It is only fair to add that Frederick, in a sincere moment, declared that Voltaire was "good to read, but a dangerous man to have anything to do with."

Before September was over, Voltaire took the liberty of informing Frederick that an enlightened prince like him was a living portrait of the divine essence. This was a little too much. "You have offered a portrait of an accomplished prince, and I cannot quite recognize myself," read the acknowledgment. Then before the year ended Frederick was as ecstatic as his partner. "I know," he wrote, "that you can't attach any price to your works; they earn their own recompense, and that is immortality. But I hope that you will be willing to accept, as a sign of my regard for you, the bust of Socrates that I am forwarding because he was the greatest of the Greeks and the master of Alcibiades."

The bust turned out to be a gold knob on a walking stick. Not that Voltaire restrained himself. "I wept tears of joy on reading you," he exclaimed. "I recognize a prince who will be loved by mankind. I am astonished. You think like Trajan, you write like Pliny, and you speak French as well as the best of our writers. What a difference there is between one man and another! Louis XIV was a great king. I respect his memory, but he did not think the humane thoughts you have, and did not always express himself so well. I have seen some of his letters. He did not know how to spell in French. Under your auspices Berlin will be the Athens of Germany and very likely of all Europe." A month passed before he discovered that Frederick's French left something to be desired. "Of course a prince shouldn't be a purist," he wrote. "But he should not write and spell *like a woman!*" Voltaire also pointed out that he did not seem to be aware of the use of commas.

In no time Frederick was begging him for instruction on the difference between poetic and nonpoetic words. To this he gave no answer, but advised him that he might improve his poetry by keeping in mind the number of syllables in the words he used. "This is the sort of comment you might receive from the janitor of the French Academy," he admitted. "But really I have no other suggestions to offer. All I can do is to sew a buckle on your shoes, while the Greeks are handing you your shirt and seeing to it that you are properly attired."

Frederick would not be discouraged. "If ever I go to France," he wrote Voltaire early in 1737, "the first thing I'll ask will be: Where is Monsieur de Voltaire? The king, the court, Paris, Versailles, women, pleasure—these things will play no part in my voyage. You alone will be important." The day was dawning when Voltaire would tell him: "I am dreaming of my prince as one dreams of one's mistress."

In the summer of 1737 Frederick could not resist sending his vivacious friend Baron Keyserlingk off to Cirey. "In taking leave of my little friend, I told him: Remember that you are going to paradise on earth, to a place that is a thousand times more enchanting than Calypso's isle, and that the goddess of that place is as beautiful as the woman who captivated Telemachus. You'll find that she has a marvelous mind, so much more desirable than mere beauty, and that this wonderful woman spends all her leisure in the search of truth."

The baron was well received at Cirey. He walked off with a bushel or two of poems and even a few fragments of the unfinished *Age of Louis XIV*. Yet he was not completely successful. "I wish I could have added *La Pucelle* to the rest of my tribute," Voltaire wrote. "Your ambassador will tell you that the thing is impossible. That little book has been for over a year in the hands of the Marquise du Châtelet, who won't let go of it."

Frederick had turned his attention to the still unpublished poem on Joan of Arc. As indecent as it was tedious, this work might have led to unpleasant repercussions with the censors. Not everyone could be amused by the many attempts to rape Joan, not to mention an ass's attempt on her virtue. "Keep that thing to yourself unless you want to be put away for the rest of your life," recommended Phélypeaux de Maurepas, Louis XV's Secretary of the Navy. When he thought of what the censors might do to him, Voltaire would cry out: "The whole world is persecuting me!"

In the fall Frederick redoubled his attentions to Emilie. "The worthy Voltaire must have known you when he composed *La Henriade,*" he wrote her, so adding a number of years to her age. "And I'd swear that the character of Queen Elizabeth is based on your own." This may not have impressed her. "The crown prince is not yet king," she had written the year before to one of Voltaire's oldest friends. "When he is, we shall both of us visit him. But until he is king, there is no guarantee. His father's only distinction is being six feet tall. He is suspicious and cruel. He hates and persecutes his son. He holds him under a yoke of iron. He is ready to believe that Monsieur de Voltaire would give him dangerous advice. He is quite capable of arresting him and handing him over to his chancellor." To the same friend she reported that Voltaire "must be saved from himself at all costs. I must be just as crafty in watching him as the Vatican is in keeping Christianity in chains."

One distinguished visitor after another was coming to Cirey. There came Francesco Algarotti, the Venetian homosexual adored by Lord Hervey in England. He was the author of *Il Neutonismo per le Dame,* in which he explained in nontechnical prose Newton's theories of light and color. Whether his visit was perfectly delightful is open to question. He began a Newtonian catechism by remarking that he was speaking neither as a marquise nor an imaginary philosopher.

Then on December 4, 1738, arrived Françoise d'Issembourg d'Happoncourt, Madame de Graffigny. She meant well but she meant panic to the household. The daughter of a lieutenant in the service of Léopold, the last duke of Lorraine, she had married the duke's chamberlain. He ended in prison and she in poverty. Her career, however, did not come to a sudden end. In 1747 she would write *la Péruvienne,* an attempt at at a novel which reached its market. She must have been rather a rattle, if we may judge by her letters to her friend Panpan, or François-Antoine Devaux, the gentleman who had the honor of reading aloud to Stanislas, the former king of Poland by now ruling over the little court at Nancy.

This should have been a happy time at Cirey, for Voltaire's *Elements of the Philosophy of Newton* had just been published at

Amsterdam. However, he was enraged by the unflattering comments of the Abbé Desfontaines, which easily put an end to his peace of mind. He was so foolish as to denounce the Abbé in the pamphlet *Le Préservatif*. This was the excuse the Abbé needed to bring out *La Voltairomanie* in December 1738, a copy of which reached Potsdam in no time.

Desfontaines was scarcely a critic. *La Voltairomanie* was a humorless condemnation of his entire career. He argued that the plays amounted to nothing: they were applauded only for their pompous tirades and their irreligious sentiments. As for *La Henriade*, it was a chaotic thing, more prose than verse, in which there were as many mistakes in French as there were pages. *Charles XII?* This was only a mediocre novel. The *Philosophical Letters?* It was just as well they were suppressed. And Voltaire's style? He was famous for his vagueness. "It is certain," Desfontaines concluded, "that if he could be cured of his insane pride, he would be less of a madman, less impious, less foolhardy, less brutal, less impetuous, less peremptory, less snide, less given to slander, less desperate, etc."

While Voltaire was taking this dreary scold seriously, Madame de Graffigny was studying the wing added to the château for his and Emilie's convenience. Here he had his reception room and his tiny bedroom tapestried in crimson velvet. And here was a room, as yet unfinished, reserved for the apparatus used for his experiments in physics. Upstairs was the small private theater, but this Madame de Graffigny overlooked. Far more important in her eyes was Emilie's bedroom, with the bed covered in watered blue silk, and the armchair, desk, and other pieces done in yellow and blue. "There is nothing quite so pretty in all the world," she decided. But since she attributed to Watteau the subjects of the paintings in the panels—presumably these were copies of things by Pater or Lancret—she was no art critic. She may have been correct when she described her own room as miserable and may have been reliable when she gave her opinion of Emilie as a housekeeper. "Except for her rooms, and Voltaire's, the house is filthy dirty," she observed.

Of course there were rewards at Cirey. Madame de Graffigny may have found Emilie tiresome when she began talking of the lawsuit that took her and Voltaire to Brussels, but one could roam through the château at liberty. She began reading the manuscript of *Louis XIV*, which Emilie had been keeping under lock and key to turn her lover from this subject. And she listened to Voltaire as he declaimed fragments of *La Pucelle*, communicating her enjoyment to her friend Panpan. This was a mistake.

After dinner on December 29, just as Madame de Graffigny was sealing a letter to Panpan, who should enter her room but Voltaire, as scrawny as ever and his eyes as electric. He was a lost man, he cried out. His life was in her hands. "How could that be?" she asked. "Why," he told her, "there must be a hundred copies in circulation of Joan's song. I'm leaving at once. I'll run away to Holland, to the end of the world. You must write at once to Panpan to recover all those copies. Is he a good enough man to oblige me?"

Madame de Graffigny said she would be only too happy to write Panpan and added that she was sorry that such a thing had happened during her stay. Upon which Voltaire fell into a rage. "You can't get out of it!" he raved. "You're the one responsible!" This went on for a good hour until Emilie made her appearance. "Here's the proof of your infamous behavior!" she screamed as she pulled out a letter and thrust it under the guilty woman's nose. "You are the most wretched of all creatures, you are a monster whom I received in my house—not because you are a friend of mine—that you never were—but because you had no place to go. And you were so vile you betrayed me! You were out to assassinate me! You stole a manuscript out of my desk to have copies made!" Emilie said much more. "She would have slapped me," Madame de Graffigny claimed, "if Voltaire hadn't dragged her away. She kept on pacing the floor, taunting me for my behavior."

Finally Madame de Graffigny insisted on seeing the fatal letter. In it was the unfortunate sentence: "Joan's song is charming." Here was salvation. All she had done, she protested, was to tell her friend how much she had enjoyed the poem. "I must say in Voltaire's favor that he believed me and begged my pardon at once."

Madame de Graffigny, who appears to have said nothing about the consequences of opening other people's mail, was later made welcome in Paris by the wife of the Duc de Richelieu. And Voltaire could comprehend that his mistress had not shown herself to advantage. "In the paradise of Cirey," he wrote Richelieu on January 12, 1739, "there is a person who will remind you of the misfortunes of this world and the generosity of your soul. I mean Madame de Graffigny, I'd break into tears over her fate if she weren't loved by you. Since that is the case, what has she to fear?" She certainly did not have to fear, as did Emilie, the indiscretion of the servants. Emilie would call in her servant Sébastien Longchamps after she had removed her chemise and was stark naked. She would also call him into the bathroom when she was in the tub.

With the explosion over Madame de Graffigny half forgotten, Voltaire turned his attention once again to the poetry of Frederick. "I imagine," he wrote him on April 15, "that you were born in the Versailles of Louis XIV, that Bossuet and Fénelon were your teachers and Madame de Sévigné your governess. However, if you desire to bow down before your miserable rules of prosody, I shall have the honor of telling Your Royal Highness that our timid writers avoid as much as possible the use of the word *croient* in poetry, because if you turn it into two syllables, it simply isn't French, and if you turn it into one syllable, it's too long."

Frederick, ever anxious to tell Voltaire how he could improve his plays by altering a line here or there, was willing to receive this advice. At one time he considered sponsoring an elegant edition of *La Henriade*, but more important was an essay of his own in French on the unwisdom of taking Machiavelli seriously. He would be an idealist, he decided, but his French, as Voltaire realized, was in need of constant improvement. One of the passages that caused some trouble was the following. "Real glory," Frederick announced, "consists in doing only good deeds, in being humane, and in calling up the troops only when one's honor is at stake, or people to be rescued from oppression, or violence checked." He added that "of all the sensations that tyrannize over one's soul, the most fatal of all is an excessive yearning for glory," a line that might have been spoken by a plaster cast.

Frederick could also not refrain from expressing his opinion of his fellow rulers in the Germanies. "Most of the little princes," he emphasized, ". . . are going deeply into debt by living beyond their means. They are drunk with their own grandeur, they will go to any length to defend the reputation of their families, and they are so vain that they are likely to end up penniless in some hospital or other. Even the youngest son of a youngest son likes to think he has something in common with Louis XIV, he has to build his Versailles, kiss his Madame de Maintenon, and keep up his army."

This was not tactful, and it is not surprising that when his father died and he ascended the throne on May 31, 1740, he decided that *L'Anti-Machiavel* had better be suppressed. This was impossible to achieve, since the book was already being printed, but Voltaire was assigned the awkward job of trying to carry out the king's orders.

Quoi! Vous êtes monarque et vous m'aimez encore! Voltaire was writing in the middle of the summer, "Socrates is on the throne and truth alone rules. He won't be searching for those giant soldiers." Perhaps the two of them might meet someplace in the Rhineland? In the presence of Emilie? But she was unnecessary, Frederick made plain. "It is you I desire to see. The divine Emilie, in all her divinity, is only an accessory to a Newtonized Apollo." Finally Frederick became obvious. "If Emilie must accompany Apollo, I agree to that, but if I can see you alone, so much the better. I'd be too much dazzled. I couldn't stand all that brightness all at once. I'd have to call on the cloud that veiled the eyes of Moses to subdue the rays of your two divinities."

"My duty must be my God," Frederick was now insisting. "Farewell to my poems and to my concerts, farewell to all my pleasures, even Voltaire." But at last, on September 11, 1740, the two met face to face in the castle of Moyland near the town of Cleves. Frederick, suffering from asthma at the time, rose from his sickbed at once. "One has to feel very well, even better than usual if that is possible," he admitted. "He has all the eloquence of Cicero, the benevolence of Pliny, and the wisdom of Agrippa. In a word he has all the virtues and all the talents of three of the greatest men of antiquity. His mind is at work every second, every drop of ink from his pen is a masterpiece of wit." So this first meeting was successful.

On the twenty-sixth of October Frederick chose to be sincere, having just heard of the death of the emperor. The fact that

Charles VI's daughter Maria Theresa had every right to claim the Austrian crown was interesting, but no more than interesting. "His death," said Frederick, "puts an end to all my thoughts of peace and I think that by next June we'll be dealing in gunpowder, soldiers, and trenches, rather than actresses, ballets, and stage performances." His eye was already on the province of Silesia, most of which he stole from Maria Theresa in the course of the War of the Austrian Succession. The war was to prove of no benefit to France, and no more than scant comfort to Maria Theresa, although she was awarded the throne. With England championing her and France her rival the Elector of Bavaria, Frederick, France's undependable partner, could play a perfectly amoral role until the Peace of Aix-la-Chapelle in 1748 brought about a truce between France and England.

"You are going to create an emperor or be one yourself," Voltaire was encouraging Frederick in the fall of 1740. "It would only be justice for the man who had the soul of the Tituses, the Trajans, and Antonines and the Julians to ascend their throne." By November, encouraged by the aging Cardinal Fleury, he was on his way to Berlin as the unofficial representative of the French government. There was not too much that he could report. It was Frederick's nature, Voltaire realized, "to always do the opposite of what he was saying or writing, not because he was double-dealing, but because he wrote or talked out of one burst of enthusiasm and then acted in response to another."

The very notion of Voltaire's setting out for Prussia was unwelcome news to Emilie. "In three weeks," she complained to Richelieu, "I've obtained for him all the privileges he had done his best to lose in the last six years. And do you know how he has repaid me for all my zeal on his behalf? When he left for Berlin, he let me know in the most matter of fact manner, well aware that he was driving a dagger into my heart. I am terribly depressed. Other people can't imagine this; only you, who have a heart, may understand."

Emilie had forgotten that Voltaire was a dramatist. Visiting Berlin for the first time was like walking into the first act of a drama whose end no one could foretell.

Frederick, and Emilie may have guessed this, was no Louis XIV. He was far from being a patron of the arts. His taste in architecture was expensive but mediocre. The great days of Potsdam would come long after he was in his grave and other Hohenzollerns would make use of the genius of Karl Friedrich Schinkel. Frederick's loyal subjects, if they had any insight, must have realized that Sans Souci, begun in 1745, did not measure up to the high standards of the Germanies in the eighteenth century. It could never be compared to the palace of Würzburg or to the Amalienburg of the Elector of Bavaria.

Did Frederick have any literary taste? This is doubtful. He was looking forward to Voltaire as an advertisement for his court, that is true, but was a most indiscriminate judge of his writings. As for Goethe, who like Schiller flourished in the last years of his reign, he was too sophisticated to resent being neglected by His Majesty. There was something comic, Goethe found, in Frederick's eager attempts to write in French. As for Lessing, too great a dramatist to preach a sermon on the subject of tolerance, he revealed all of its charm in *Nathan The Wise* in 1779 while Frederick was still on the throne. But this meant nothing at all in Potsdam where no one understood that German was about to become one of the great languages of the world.

Was Frederick a genuine patron of music? This too is doubtful, although it seems likely that he was an accomplished flutist. Quantz and Graun, whose names are familiar only to musicologists, were the composers he favored; he wrote the libretto for an opera by the latter, but the opera itself is no more than a curiosity. It is true that he counted for twenty-seven years on the services of Karl Philip Emanuel Bach as accompanist, and that Karl had the honor of playing the harpsichord at the first flute concert of His Majesty on inheriting the throne. But Karl Bach cannot be said to have been richly rewarded. Much of the time he was paid in paper currency which quickly became worthless. Nor did Karl's father Johann Sebastian Bach have any reason to be grateful. Ordered to write some variations on a theme supplied by Frederick, he got no money at all for the *Musical Offering*.

Even in the few days Voltaire spent in Berlin on this his first trip, he could appreciate the fact that the court had a character of its own. No clergymen were tolerated in the royal palace. Voltaire may not have missed them. Nor were any women allowed. Although the king had been married to the Princess Elisabeth of

Brunswick-Wolfenbüttel, he did not choose to live with her, and his one attempt to keep a mistress came to nothing. There was a time when he saw something of a schoolteacher's daughter who played the harpsichord rather badly while he accompanied her on the flute. "He thought he was in love with her," Voltaire remarked, "but he was wrong. He had no vocation for the other sex."

Frederick's father, who loathed all things French and doted on the giants he was recruiting for the Prussian army, had this mistress whipped in public by the executioner. He was never one to humor his son. "He knows," he said, "that I can't abide an effeminate fellow who has no inclination worthy to be called human." He could not have been surprised to learn that his son was planning to run away with two friends. One of them escaped to Portugal. The other, Hans Hermann von Katte, was apprehended, kicked and caned by His Majesty, and after being court-martialed, sentenced to life imprisonment. But the king decided that he must have his head cut off and that Frederick must observe the carrying out of the sentence. "I am ready to renounce my right to the crown," Frederick protested, "if His Majesty will pardon Katte." This could not be, and Frederick fainted at the sight of the ax. He was then given strict orders neither to speak nor write in French.

The only woman Frederick may be said to have respected was his sister Wilhelmina, the Margravine of Bayreuth. She was a bully in her own right and her greatest joy was in humiliating a younger sister. Quite naturally, she was suspected of conniving in Frederick's flight to freedom. Her father was about to throw her out of a window when her mother dared to intervene, grabbing her by the skirt. She got an ugly bruise above the left breast. "This," noted Voltaire, "she bore all her life as a mark of paternal affection, and she did me the honor of showing it."

Frederick could now scarcely resist exhibiting all the Watteaus, Lancrets, and Paters he had acquired for his art gallery. "I have seen all this," Voltaire wrote a friend, "but I suspect that the four little examples of Watteau he keeps in his study are excellent copies."

Before the year was over Voltaire was writing Frederick about his new tragedy, *Mahomet ou le Fanatisme*. "Your Majesty knows very well the mood I was in while composing this work. My pen was guided by my love of mankind and my horror of fanaticism, two virtues that will ever be cherished by your throne." He had thought of dedicating the drama to Frederick, but in the end decided that the amiable Pope Benedict XIV should have the honor. The Pope was pleased to write him a letter praising his poetry, incidentally pointing out an error in his Latin.

Mahomet was a success in Lille on its opening night in 1741. Between the acts arrived a letter from Frederick telling of his victory at Mollwitz on the tenth of April. This Voltaire read out loud to the audience. There was applause. "You will see," he told Frederick, "that this play at Mollwitz will insure the success of my own play." *Mahomet* might have been a hit in Paris the next year had it not, after three performances, been taken off the stage by the authorities, who discovered that here was a play denouncing not Mahomet but Jesus Christ. This was the opinion of Lord Chesterfield, who heard Voltaire one evening recite the drama in Brussels. "I was suprised," said Chesterfield, "that no one noticed this at Lille. What I can't forgive, and what can't be forgiven, is all the trouble he is taking to propagate a doctrine so pernicious to society and so contrary to religion everywhere."

"Le Salomon du Nord en est l'Alexandre?" wrote Voltaire to Frederick, congratulating him on his victory over the Austrians at Chotusitz on May 17, 1742. This triumph was recognized on the twelfth of June by Maria Theresa, who by the Treaty of Breslau surrendered both Upper and Lower Silesia. Frederick, and this will surprise no one, lost no time in losing interest in the fate of his French allies. This was the very moment that Voltaire selected to hail Frederick as "the peacemaker of Germany and of all Europe. It is my opinion," he told him on June 30, "that you have been too quick for that kind old man"—a reference to Louis XV's minister Cardinal Fleury. This letter was not ignored in Paris. "Have you heard the latest news?" Madame du Deffand was asked. "It's that letter of Voltaire to the king of Prussia, the craziest thing you can imagine." This was all very embarrassing; to save himself Voltaire prevailed upon Frederick to write him questioning the authenticity of the message of June 30.

In the fall of 1742 Voltaire met Frederick at Aachen with Fleury's blessing. Could he possibly penetrate Frederick's intentions? "I have seen the king of Prussia," he reported to his old friend the Marquis d'Argenson, soon to be appointed Minister of Foreign Affairs. "And I've seen him in a way kings are seldom seen, completely at my ease, in my own room by the fireside, where the very same man who has won two battles talked in as friendly a manner to me as Scipio to Terence." The French government was apparently pleased by the result of this conference, although it amounted to nothing.

But this was all the invitation Voltaire needed to play a role at Potsdam that appealed to his sense of humor. If the French government could be persuaded to persecute him, he could turn up at the Prussian court as a refugee. Versailles was willing to oblige. His latest play, La Mort de César, scheduled to be performed by the Comédie Française, was suddenly withdrawn in June 1743. This was gratifying to Frederick. "Voltaire," he announced, "is getting out of France for good." If only he could be ensnared. "My intention," he told his ambassador to Paris, Count von Rothenburg, "is to get Voltaire in so much trouble in France that the only way out will be for him to come and stay with us." He also circulated a poem in French that he attributed to Voltaire, in which Louis XV was described as "the most stupid of kings."

In no real danger of trusting to Frederick's kindness, Voltaire was revolted in the fall of 1743 by this exhibit of His Majesty's diplomacy. "Since he can't get me any other way, he thinks he can acquire me by ruining my reputation in France," he wrote Amelot de Chaillou at court, "but I swear I'd rather settle down in some Swiss city rather than enjoy, at such a price, the favor of a king capable of bringing the element of treachery into friendship." Whether he enlightened the foreign office by the reports he sent back from Potsdam is a question, but he seems to have enjoyed himself. He was also so tactful as to pay a call on Wilhelmina at Bayreuth. The great world remained the great world.

Emilie, who complained that her lover had not written her a word in two weeks, did not realize the pleasure he took in watching what was going on. At Potsdam he could inspect La Barbarina, the Italian dancer Frederick had kidnapped from Venice. "He was a little in love with her," Voltaire remarked, "because she had the legs of a man."

His Majesty was his father's son, no matter if he played the flute every evening and devoted most of the afternoon to writing poems in French. He would rise at five in summer, no later than six in winter, and every day at eleven would review the regiment of his guards. The colonels stationed elsewhere in the kingdom were bound to review their men at the identical hour. As for the food served at the royal table, it was wretched, which was not extraordinary, since Prussia was a land that could furnish no game, no passable meat of any kind, not even a chicken. However, the conversation at dinner was curious. The king and his favorites were free to discuss with unbelievable freedom all the superstitions in which men were taught to believe. "God was respected," Voltaire claimed, "but those who deceived mankind in His name were not spared."

Court for court, Versailles was more attractive than Potsdam, no matter if Louis XV was neither widely read nor even gracious. "You're looking awfully old," he told one aging courtier. "Where do you want to be buried?" "At your feet, Sire," came the answer.

However, on the twenty-eighth of February 1745, while attending a masked ball, Louis XV had the presence of mind to pick up a handkerchief dropped by a certain Madame Lenormant d'Etioles. She was the daughter of a kept woman and an embezzler who had to flee the country, but she was, Voltaire perceived, "very well educated, born with good sense and a good heart. Moreover, she was talented, amiable, and kind." Here was the future Madame de Pompadour.

Although her mortal enemy was Voltaire's friend Richelieu, this did not mean that she was banned from Voltaire's horizon. He could sympathize with the awful responsibility she assumed for preserving Louis XV from boredom. His cheeks would acquire a yellow tinge when he was bored, a symptom that she never failed to recognize. Voltaire could also admire her tact. When presented to the queen, she said: "I have the greatest passion to please you." Never given to mean remarks, she was a grateful beauty. When she became the king's mistress, she did not forget a certain Madame Lebon, who prophesied, when she was nine, that she would get her wish. A pension of £60 a year was Madame Lebon's reward.

No one could prove that Madame de Pompadour was an intellectual, but she had the taste to discern that Boucher should remind the future of her features. He painted her again and again, and a version of his *Toilet of Venus* was hanging in her bathroom. Her instinct for the decorative arts was sure: she called on Huet, when she rented the château of Champs from the Duc de la Vallière, to improve the setting with his chinoiseries. As for Gabriel, she recognized his genius, devoting some of her own savings to the completion of the Ecole Militaire, and asking him to create for her own use the exquisite Hermitage at Fontainebleau. Finally, weary of the continuing success of the pottery of Dresden, she founded the Sèvres works that ensured the supremacy of France.

Visiting her at Champs, Voltaire was moved to write:

> *Quand César, cet héros charmant,*
> *Dont tout Rome fut idolâtre,*
> *Gagnait quelque combat brillant,*
> *On en faisait compliment*
> *A la divine Cléopâtre.*

> *Quand Louis, cet héros charmant,*
> *Dont tout Paris fait son idole,*
> *Gagne quelque combat brillant,*
> *On en doit faire compliment*
> *A la divine Etiole*

[*When Caesar, that charming hero,/Whom all Rome idolized,/Won some brilliant battle,/People would compliment/The Divine Cleopatra./When Louis, that charming hero,/Idolized by all Paris,/Wins some brilliant battle,/We should compliment/The divine Etiole.*]

The battle of Fontenoy, won by the Maréchal de Saxe on the eleventh of May 1745 on the fields of Flanders, may not have been the most important engagement of the War of the Austrian Succession, but it was a victory—a victory won in the very presence of Louis XV—and may have partly erased the memory of the defeat at Dettingen two years before. The Dettingen *Te Deum* was

Händel's chance. Fontenoy was Voltaire's, and he wrote a proper if hardly memorable poem on the occasion. The Maréchal de Saxe reported to Emilie that the king was quite satisfied. "In fact, he told me that the work was above criticism." Voltaire was not displeased to hear this. "You may imagine," he wrote, "that from now on I must believe that the king is the best and greatest connoisseur of the realm." Which proved that he could forgive and forget. Only six years before this, the opening chapters of the *Age of Louis XIV* had been seized and suppressed by His Majesty's censors.

But Voltaire had every right to expect a warm reception from Madame de Pompadour. "I knew her very well," he claimed, thinking back to the days when she went riding, dressed in pink, in the forest of Sénart. "She trusted me with the secret of her love." She was the one who proposed he collaborate with Rameau on the *Temple de la Gloire*, an opera-ballet to celebrate Fontenoy once more.

This libretto was one of Voltaire's efforts, not one of his achievements, but there could be no doubt that he was rising in the world. With Madame de Pompadour at the king's elbow, he was received into the French Academy on the sixth of May 1746. Montesquieu, whose admiration for Voltaire was occasionally restrained, allowed that his election was inevitable. "He isn't handsome," he pointed out. "He is only pretty. It would be a disgrace for the Academy if he were in it, and some day it will be ashamed of not inviting him."

The address that Voltaire delivered was commonplace. After paying tribute to the dramas of Corneille, he went on to inundate Frederick with compliments on his French and then was worse than obsequious on the subject of Louis XV. "If his enemies," he argued, "could ever recognize the goodness of his heart, they would let him settle all disputes instead of going to war, and that might be the only way of taking advantage of him."

Before the year was over, Voltaire was appointed historiographer to the king and made Gentleman of the Chamber, a £60,000 sinecure that he was permitted to sell off at a profit. So he was not overlooked, even though he complained, recalling the *Princesse de Navarre*, a skit he and Rameau had worked on for the dauphin's wedding, that "honors have rained down upon me for a mere farce for a fair."

Voltaire's history of the battles of 1741, like his review of the reign of Louis XV, may be skipped by those who refuse to prize his every page. These were, after all, merely the assignments he fulfilled as historiographer. Madame de Pompadour was of course everywhere. Trained in declamation by the aging dramatist Crébillon, she took the role of Lise in a court production of Voltaire's comedy *L'Enfant Prodigue.*

A compliment was in order. There came this from Voltaire:

> *Ainsi donc, vous réunissez*
> *Tous les arts, tous les goûts, tous les talents de plaire*
> *Pompadour, vous embellissez*
> *La cour, le Parnasse et Cythère.*
> *Charme de tous les coeurs, trèsor d'un seul mortel,*
>
> *Qu'un sort si beau soit éternel!*
> *Que vos jours précieux soient marqués par des fêtes!*
> *Que la paix dans nos champs revienne avec Louis!*
> *Soyes tous deux sans ennemis,*
> *Et tous deux gardez vos conquêtes.*

[*Thus you unite/All the arts, all tastes, all pleasing talents/Pompadour, you adorn/The court, Parnassus, and Cythera./Charm of all hearts, treasure of a single mortal,/Oh that a life so beautiful be eternal!/Oh that your precious days be marked by celebrations!/Oh that with Louis peace return to our fields!/Oh that the two of you be without enemies, And you both preserve your victories.*]

These and other sweet nothings may have pleased Madame de Pompadour, but the reference to keeping one's conquests could not have seemed tactful to the queen. If one were to be a success at court, one had to be watchful.

Watchful was not the word for Emilie, so intent on discovering errors in the Bible that she seldom thought of what impression she might be making. There came that day when she decided to accompany Voltaire to Fontainebleau. The queen set aside three carriages for herself and her ladies. Emilie showed up a little ahead of time and settled herself in the first vehicle available without ever thinking that she might be wise to take her turn. Whereupon three of the ladies took their places in another carriage, leaving her by herself. When she attempted to join the three, she was told there was no room and so was obliged to make the journey alone. The Duc de Luynes, so close to the queen, remarked in his memoirs that "Madame du Châtelet was filled with the grandeur of her family, and ever conscious of her rights, presuming that the first place would be forever hers." Emilie did apologize for her behavior to Madame de Luynes, who conveyed her excuses to the queen, but the incident was not forgotten.

Emilie was even more indiscreet one evening playing cards in the queen's company. She lost four hundred louis, which was all the money she had on her person, and Voltaire, who had only two hundred louis with him, borrowed another two hundred at interest. This was not all. Emilie kept on playing and was eighty-four thousand francs in debt when the evening was over. "You've been playing with card sharks," Voltaire told her in English. This was not only overheard but understood by the other guests. The two were not so safe as they had believed.

All this made the invitation of the mischievous Duchesse du Maine to spend a few days at the château of Anet so welcome. The two of them turned up toward midnight on the fourteenth of August 1747 and were greeted by the patient Rose de Staal-Delaunay, the duchess's devoted companion. Her memoirs reveal all the command of self that a woman might exhibit in eighteenth-century France.

She was far from patient, however, when it came to Emilie. She saw no reason to disguise her feelings in her letters to Madame du Deffand, who had, as we have seen, her own reservations on this subject.

"They showed up," Rose wrote, "like two ghosts, and they smelled like two embalmed bodies dug out of the grave. We were just finishing dinner. But the ghosts were famished, they had to eat, and besides, the beds were not made up for them." During the day the two were not to be seen. Rose surmised that one was busy transcribing important facts, the other perfecting her commentary on Newton. They wouldn't take any walks, and they wouldn't play any games. "They really did not amount to much in a society where their learned contributions were out of place."

Five days later Rose reported that Emilie had moved out of her room. "She couldn't put up with the one she had first selected. It was noisy and smoky even though there was no fire. (Smoke without any fire may be her distinguishing characteristic.) As for the noise, it didn't bother her by night but in the day time, when she was hard at work. It interrupted her train of thought. She is now reviewing the state of the principles on which she stands. This is an exercise she repeats every year; otherwise her ideas might get away from her—so far away that she might never find one of them again. I really believe that her brain is a sort of house of correction, and not the place where her ideas are born . . . Voltaire has been writing a few polite verses, which does something to make up for the peculiar conduct of both of them."

A little later Rose was telling Madame du Deffand that they were holding a room for her—the very one Emilie had been occupying. "You'll find a little less furniture than she required, for she rummaged through every single room she spent the night in to furnish this one. She had six or seven tables installed, she had to have them in all sizes to spread out her papers, besides substantial tables for her luggage and toilet articles and something less imposing for her jewelry and her tassels."

Perhaps it was just as well that Emilie did not accompany Voltaire when he visited the duchess at Sceaux a few weeks after this. There he kept to his room for weeks on end, often emerging at two in the morning to dine with the duchess in her bedroom, now and then entertaining her by reading aloud the tales that were a kind of prelude to *Candide*. He also listened with understandable eagerness to the duchess's anecdotes of life at Versailles under Louis XIV.

This last amusement, this last freedom seems to have come to an end when Emilie finally rejoined him. But plays were performed, and since his *Prude* was put on the stage with Emilie in the cast, he saw no reason why this admittedly insignificant piece should not be advertised as though it were worthy of his reputation. A circular was drawn up:

On Friday, December 15 new actors will present, at the Sceaux theater, a new five-act comedy in verse. Everyone is invited to come, without ceremony. You must be on hand exactly at six, and order your carriage to be in the courtyard by seven-thirty or eight. After six o'clock no one will be admitted.

The duchess, who was not consulted about all this, seems to have been displeased by the crowds that invaded her domain. In any event, by the first of February 1748 Voltaire and Emilie moved on to Lunéville in Lorraine to enjoy the hospitality of Stanislas, the former king of Poland. Although the glory of Stanislas's Nancy, the Place Stanislas invented by Emmanuel Héré and Jean Lamour, had not yet been erected, Lunéville could be compared as a château to Sceaux, for it had been designed years before this by Germain Boffrand for the last duke of Lorraine. Stanislas himself was an amiable man, even if the court dwarf, Bébé, fifteen inches tall, was too proud of his skill in leaping out of the rich pâtés set before the king's guests. There were twenty-nine men on the staff of the *service de la bouche*, and Gilles, the master chef, was renowned for the quality of his desserts.

Voltaire confessed that at Lunéville he was living in an enchanted castle. Moreover, more than one of his plays was being staged and Emilie was displaying her talent as an actress. Yet he was not without his worries. He was laboring at this time on *Sémiramis*, a drama that he was convinced would conquer Paris, and he accompanied Stanislas to Paris for the first night. The play won only a modest success and, what was equally embarrassing, had to be censored by Crébillon, who had already written a play of his own on this subject. Voltaire was positive that his rival's *Sémiramis* was "the work of a madman written by a fool, and as a matter of fact, you can't find a more mediocre writer than he is."

There was the threat that a parody of Voltaire's *Sémiramis* would be presented. The news made him nervous, and he prevailed upon Stanislas to have the queen, his daughter, suppress this annoyance. On the opening night of his play he slunk off to the Café Procope to eavesdrop on any and all comments. They could not have been too favorable.

However, a greater disappointment than the reception of *Sémiramis* was waiting for him early in October 1748, when he and Emilie were staying at Commercy in Lorraine, the vast if not exactly splendid château by Nicolas Dorby that Stanislas had placed at their disposal. Quite by chance Voltaire interrupted Emilie on the sofa with Jean-François, Marquis de Saint-Lambert, a thirty-one-year-old soldier who passed for a poet at the court of Stanislas. The two were discussing something besides poetry or philosophy, so the valet Longchamps has told us.

The time had come for Voltaire to master the art of composure. He succeeded, but his humiliation was obvious. Saint-Lambert had not been noticed before this, possibly because Voltaire was not in the habit of reading Emilie's correspondence. "I have been doing all the loving for both of us," she had complained to one of Voltaire's oldest friends. Once she and Saint-Lambert became intimate, she used an abandoned harp as the letterbox for her notes.

Voltaire's fury was real at finding Emilie with her new lover, and her attempt to persuade him that he had not seen what he had was futile. She then reminded him that he was fifty-four. This was clever of her, for in 1741 he had written her a poem that would touch on his predicament in 1748:

> *Si vous voulez que j'aime encore*
> *Rendez-moi l'âge des amours . . .*

[*If you want me to keep on loving/Give me back the age in which one falls in love . . .*]

"Ah, Madame," he decided, "you will always be in the right. But since this is the way things stand, I don't want to see what is going on." A little later he made up with Saint-Lambert. "My child," he told him, "I have forgotten all this. I was the one in the wrong. You are at that happy time when one falls in love and makes a conquest and you should enjoy yourself all you can. A sick man, an old man like me, isn't really meant to have a good time."

He was not telling the exact truth, but the exact truth would not have been pleasing to Emilie. Four years before this he had found that his sister's daughter, Marie-Louise Denis, was irresistible. The passion he spent on her may be documented in the many letters he had been writing her. She was a canny woman, the widow of a notary who may have educated her in bookkeeping. She was determined to be comfortable in this world and saw no reason why Voltaire should not pay in full for the privilege of enjoying her plump person.

And since he was satisfied, he was not unduly disturbed, early in December, to learn that Emilie was pregnant by Saint-Lambert. The Marquis du Châtelet was summoned to receive the comic homage due him as the presumed father, and a very good time was had by everyone—with the possible exception of the two children born twenty years ago or more to her and the Marquis. The two young people may well have wondered what the newcomer would do to their interest in the family property.

Emilie, forty-two at the time her pregnancy could no longer be concealed, must have shared now and then in the misgivings of her children. She began to wonder whether she could count on Saint-Lambert to be faithful. She reproached him again and again for his disloyalty. Early in January 1749 she was telling him: "You can put an end to everything with one word, and you won't tell me what I want to hear. The word is: *you love me.*" Come April she was plaguing him: "I've told you I'm pregnant. Are you turning away from me?" Later in the month she was muttering: "I'll go to have my baby in Lorraine, even though my heart is aware of all the distinctions between the way you love me now and the way you used to love me."

Frederick, who knew nothing of her fears, was no friend of hers in her predicament. "Madame du Châtelet is having a baby in September," he wrote Voltaire in June 1749. "You are not a midwife, and she can easily have her child without your assistance." This comment was so direct that Voltaire gave a direct answer. "I haven't got her with child," he protested. "Nor am I a doctor or a midwife. But I am a friend of hers, and I couldn't abandon, even for Your Majesty, a woman who may die in the month of September."

She did die in September, in fact on the tenth, and at Lunéville. A week before this she had given birth to a little girl who did not have long to live. Writing about her birthpangs to an old school friend, Voltaire mentioned that she had been at her desk, scribbling away about Newton, when she had to relieve herself. "Upon which a little girl made her appearance. We laid her out on top of a treatise on geometry. In the meantime the mother has gone to bed, and if she weren't sound asleep, would be writing you herself this minute. As for me, I have just given birth to a tragedy dealing with Catiline, and am a thousand times more tired than she is. All she has done is to bring into the world a little girl who can't speak a word, and I, I've had to bring Cicero and Caesar back to life, and it's much harder to set them talking than to produce a baby."

He was more serious when telling Madame Denis of Emilie's death. Serious and honest. "I had given up thinking of Madame du Châtelet as a woman, you know that, and I hope you may appreciate the extent of my grief." He could not forgive himself, he confided to Madame du Deffand, for saluting the birth of Emilie's child with good humor. To Saint-Lambert he railed: "You are the one who killed her! Why did you have to get her with child?"

The day would come for him to write a eulogy of Emilie, praising the precision of her mind and her other excellent qualities. The immediate problem was personal. When he went over her correspondence, he discovered that she had been faithless again and again. Not only that, but she had removed his portrait from her ring and substituted that of Saint-Lambert. This was in order, he had to admit, for he had seen his portrait take the place of that of the Duc de Richelieu.

Voltaire was not heartbroken, but a change of scenery was called for. On July 10, 1750, he arrived in Potsdam, alone. It would have been pleasant if Madame Denis had come along. Frederick, however, did not encourage this suggestion. "I shall be happy to see Madame Denis accompany you, but I am not requiring her presence," he made plain. There was no ceremony when Voltaire took his leave of Louis XV. The king simply turned his shoulder. It was obvious that he would not be missed at Versailles. "I've treated him just as well as Louis XIV treated Racine and Boileau," Louis XV reflected. "As we have a few more great intellects and great lords than there are in Prussia, I'd have to set up a long, long table to accomodate all of them."

Voltaire had been planning the *Age of Louis XIV* for many years. At the Prussian court he would have every opportunity to compare the dead king of France to the living King of Prussia. The move might be worthwhile.

4

THE SONG OF SOLOMON

Potsdam promised to be an adventure. However, Voltaire was not to rejoice that Frederick had left the natural use of women, and the womanless paradise of Sans Souci was bound to be boring sooner or later. Quite possibly sooner. For Frederick also had a profound weakness for the company of atheists, whose opinions, thought Voltaire, were rarely worth hearing. Furthermore, in this respect his father's son, Frederick was a merciless tease. Even though he presented Voltaire with the highest Prussian order, *Pour le Mérite*, and made him his chamberlain with a pension of twenty thousand pounds a year, he could not resist embarrassing him.

So he invited the insignificant poet François-Thomas-Marie de Baculard d'Arnaud to join the court. Once the lover of Madame Denis, he had once been befriended by Voltaire. This was all the excuse Frederick required to proclaim that the Apollo of France was entering into his decline. "Come and shine in your turn!" he hailed Baculard, who quickly became impossible and had to be dismissed. "D'Arnaud has behaved badly toward you," Frederick admitted to Voltaire. "A generous man would have forgiven him these wrongs; a vindictive man persecutes those whom he hates. In short, although d'Arnaud has not harmed me, it is because of you that he left."

What was Voltaire to think of all this? He would change his mind again and again about Potsdam, but was close to a final judgment when he told Madame Denis toward the end of his first year that this was not "a court, but a refuge from which all women are banished."

The British ambassador extraordinary, Sir Charles Hanbury Williams, would have agreed. His preference for women was well known long before he contracted the syphilis that drove him, insane, to the ministrations of Dr. Batty. To Hanbury Williams Voltaire was "vainer than any other Frenchman." Yet he had a certain pity for him in his role as one of the "He-Muses that adorn this German Parnassus, for no female is allowed to approach this court. Males wash the linen, nurse the children, make and unmake the beds."

In the eyes of Hanbury Williams Frederick was "the completest tyrant that God ever sent for a scourge to an offending people . . . There is nothing here but an absolute prince and a people, all equally miserable, all equally trembling before him, and all equally detesting his iron government . . . The thing His Prussian Majesty has in the greatest abhorrence is matrimony. No man, however great a favorite, must think of it. If he does, he is certain never to be preferred."

Perhaps the British ambassador extraordinary was guilty of a slight exaggeration in regard to Frederick's lack of enthusiasm for the married state. Now and then one of his favorites was allowed to take a wife. Jean-Baptiste de Boyer, Marquis d'Argens, for example, finally honored the actress who shared his bed. But he was an incorrigible adventurer who got into trouble almost everywhere upon leaving his native Aix. A misfit famous in his day for his antireligious pamphlets, he could be excused for this one deviation from the Potsdam code. He was even presented with a house of his own, decorated, it is true, with paintings portraying the most shameful incidents of his career. These paintings he had rubbed out after proving to His Majesty that he could swallow almost any practical joke. In the end this friendship cooled. Was there one practical joke too many? Or was the sight of his wife more than Frederick could bear?

Another great favorite was Julien Offray de La Mettrie, a native of Saint-Malo who became a complete aetheist after mastering the intricacies of Jansenist theology. He was also a physician, devoting much of his time to the study of venereal diseases. *L'Homme Machine* is the correct title of his most famous work. In his company Frederick was perfectly at ease. In fact he told him, referring to Voltaire: "I'll need him for another year or so at most. Once you've squeezed the orange, you throw the skin away." Voltaire was to ponder, on hearing this remark, the generosity of his royal patron. "You may tell me: get out," he wrote his niece, "but I can't say it's time to leave. When you have begun something, you must finish it." He was hard at work on his own projects. "What can I do? I can forget that La Mettrie told me this, confide only in you, and see what's going to happen." He was still thinking about the orange skin when the corpse of La Mettrie, swollen big as a barrel, was carried into the local Catholic church. He had never been a dainty feeder. He died of stuffing himself with an entire pheasant pie that had been fattened with rancid bacon, pork hash, and ginger. Frederick was pleased to note that he died not a Christian but a philosopher. "I am very happy," he explained, "for the repose of his soul."

These were the days when Voltaire was laboring manfully to correct and alter His Majesty's French verses. Hanbury Williams, watching him at work, heard him say "he wished with all his heart they were thrown into the fire." Frederick's sister, the Margravine of Bayreuth, could not have lightened the poet's load—at least if Hanbury Williams is to be trusted. "There is a Bitch Royal for you," he declared. "Besides all this, she is an atheist, and talks about fate and destiny, and makes a joke of a future state . . . I never saw a woman so learn'd ignorant or so seriously foolish in all my life."

We do not know what Hanbury Williams thought of Algarotti, the dabbler in Newton who courted Frederick in the days when he was crown prince, but it was evident that Algarotti could be important if he wished. In the year before Voltaire settled down in Potsdam, Algarotti was told just what to think of him. "It is a shame," said Frederick, "that such a coward can have so much genius. He is as nice as a monkey and just as malicious . . . You can learn a lot from a crook. I want him to teach me French. What do I care about his morals?"

Yet another important figure at the court was François-Egmont de Chasot, a native of Caen who liked women more than Frederick thought necessary, but had saved his master's life in the battle of Mollwitz by impersonating him. He was also a competent flutist, which more than compensated for certain blemishes in his military record. He had killed a man in a duel while serving in the French army of the Rhine. This led him to desert, and he hacked the skull off a Polish major while in the Prussian service. For this he was sentenced to a year in Spandau prison, remitted, thanks to Frederick, to a few weeks.

Larger than Chasot loomed Maupertuis, the president of the Academy at Berlin, whom Voltaire had suggested for that post. Trouble with Maupertuis was indicated even before the day a certain General Manstein stopped by Voltaire's apartment to ask after his *Memoirs of Russia*, a book Manstein hoped Voltaire would put into French. "Let us leave off for the present, my friend, you see the king has sent me his dirty linen to wash. I will wash yours another time." The comment was to be repeated to His Majesty by Maupertuis.

In the meantime all was well. Day after day Voltaire improved His Majesty's verses and even gave his advice on another project, a history of Prussia to be written in French. Voltaire's plays were also royally performed. "People in Paris," he wrote his niece late in 1750, "should know that we have staged *La Mort de César*." Once *Zaïre* and *Rome Sauvée* were added to the repertory and Prince Henry proved to be a good actor with no German accent whatever, he could begin to feel that the tiresome journey through the vast, morbid, sterile, and detestable plains of Westphalia was worth the effort.

In fact he was occasionally too happy for words. A dangerous state of mind, that, for someone who could use the language. He told one close friend that Frederick "doesn't send me to the salt mines for criticizing his verses, he thanks me, and he makes the necessary corrections." He never could forget that Louis XV had simply looked the other way when informed that he was accepting Frederick's invitation. "I was lured away by the entreaties and prayers of a king who has some reputation in the world," he reminded the Duc de Richelieu. "Madame de Pompadour can do all she likes to promote mediocre poets, mediocre musicians, and mediocre painters, and what do I care?" Besides, there were no priests to be found in the gardens of Sans Souci. "My kingdom is not of this world," he pointed out to Madame du Deffand's great friend the Duc de Choiseul. "If I'd stayed in Paris, I'd have fallen sick and they would have asked me to make my confession."

Was he struggling to convince himself when writing Madame du Deffand? "When a new book comes out in Paris that is presumed to be clever but is really a collection of chestnuts in a new binding, do you know what we do here? We don't read it. All the good books of the last century may be had right here, and that is just as it should be." In another letter he told her: "When one has the misfortune in Paris to be a public character, such as I was, do you know the only thing to do? Run away . . . Just imagine how pleasant it is to be a free man in a king's household, to think, write, and say anything one pleases. You were all of you slaves at Sceaux and Anet, yes, slaves, compared with the liberty we enjoy at Potsdam."

In this same mood he wrote the Margravine of Bayreuth that it was difficult to know her brother without loving him. "He is one of those phenomena who make their appearance only once in a century, at best." But this was the very man who would not supply Voltaire with coffee, tea, and chocolate of the quality to which he was accustomed. It was evident that the hospitality of Potsdam was inadequate. Bored, Voltaire was ready to indulge in one of his oldest habits, speculation.

On November 23, 1750, he called upon Abraham Hirschel, a Jew known for his talent in making money in forbidden transactions, and requested him to buy up for his account in Dresden a certain amount of Saxon bonds. These were then selling at thirty-five per cent below par, but according to a Prussian-Saxon treaty, could be redeemed at par by Prussians. This was such an easy invitation to attack the Saxon treasury that Frederick, on the eighth of May 1748 agreed that the bonds could no longer be imported. Despite this, Voltaire went ahead. Offering a bill of exchange on Paris for forty-thousand francs and a draft on a Berlin Jew for four thousand shillings, he made Hirschel his agent. As agent, Hirschel turned over certain diamonds as security. But then Voltaire saw fit to cancel the bill of exchange that Hirschel cashed, and a nasty quarrel followed, with Hirschel demanding the return of his diamonds. Voltaire lost his temper, snatched a ring off Hirschel's finger, and the affair had to be settled in court.

Voltaire kept at it, but not without making himself ridiculous. "Brother Voltaire is doing penance," he wrote the Margravine of Bayreuth. "There's a nasty case with a Jew, and according to the law of the Old Testament, he'll have to pay up for having been cheated."

Frederick was not pleased, and the dignity with which he behaved on this occasion was, for once, kingly. He would not allow Voltaire in his presence until the case was settled. He knew that Voltaire was lying when he claimed he had sent Hirschel to Dresden to buy furs and diamonds and was irritated by his language. "If I have to go to court with a Jew," Voltaire complained, "that is simply my hard luck . . . I have not lived to my present age without having my share of suffering, but the happiness of loving you is a great consolation."

"I had thought," Frederick answered, "that a man of your age, sick and tired of quarreling with authors and exposing himself to thunderstorms, had come here to take refuge in a quiet harbor . . . You've been involved in the ugliest business in the world with a Jew . . . Until you came, I kept the peace in my house, and I warn you, that if you insist on scheming and plotting, you've come to the wrong place. I like gentle and peaceable people who don't struggle with the violent passions of tragedies. In the event you make up your mind to live like a philosopher, I shall be pleased to see you. But if you give way to tantrums and have it in for everybody, you won't be doing me any favor by coming here, and you might as well stay in Berlin." His reception in Potsdam was left in doubt. Later on Frederick made plain that he hoped Voltaire would cease wrangling with both the Old and the New Testament.

The Margravine of Bayreuth understood that her brother had the upper hand. "What extraordinary news you give me," she wrote Voltaire. "Apollo going to court with a Jew! Fie upon you, sir, that is abominable. I've run through all my mythologies, and have not come across any case like this in Parnassus. I hope your Jew will pay the penalty for his crooked dealings, and that you may calm down."

There was nothing to do but apologize. "Your Majesty is right," Voltaire wrote Frederick. "I was absolutely in the wrong. I never have recovered from the silly idea that I should always have my way, and although I realize that there are a thousand occasions when you must lose and keep quiet, and even though I was aware of all that, I had to prove my point . . . I am in despair, I've never felt any affliction so deep and so bitter. In a careless moment I've deprived myself of the reason for which I came here. I have stopped enjoying all the conversation that would have enlightened me and brought me back to life. I have displeased the only man I wanted to please."

Although Voltaire insisted that he had behaved with a generosity not found in the Old Testament, he had shown that tolerance was an ideal in which he could not believe every day in the week. This lesson was not lost upon Gotthold Ephraim Lessing, the twenty-two-year-old German he hired as translator during the trial. "German," thought Voltaire, "is for soldiers and horses; it is only necessary when you are on the road."

Lessing, who made the mistake of borrowing a copy of the *Age of Louis XIV*, whose first edition, in French, came out in Berlin in December 1751, found he was accused of stealing the book for the purpose of publishing an unauthorized German translation. Voltaire fell into a rage. This was unfortunate, for Lessing, a shrewd critic as well as an important dramatist, dissected Voltaire's *Sémiramis* with joy and proved that his *Mérope* owed all too much to its source, a play of the same title by the Italian Maffei. "What good does it do to find fault with Voltaire?" asked Lessing. "He speaks, and people believe him." He seems to have suspected that for all his success at the moment Voltaire was at best stale on stage and could never recapture the glow of either Corneille or Racine. It may not be unfair to point out that the author of *Nathan the Wise* associated with more distinguished Jews than Abraham Hirschel. One of Lessing's close friends was the philosopher Moses Mendelssohn, the grandfather of the composer.

But enough about the Hirschel case. With the *Age of Louis XIV* Voltaire became the great historian of his century. Lord Chesterfield, so pompous in giving advice to his natural son, displayed an unnatural talent for book reviewing in his comments. "It is," he said, "the history of the human understanding, written by a man of parts, for the use of men of parts. Weak minds will not like it, even though they do not understand it; which is commonly the measure of their admiration. Dull ones will want those minute and uninteresting details with which most other histories are encumbered. He tells me all I want to know, and nothing more."

"*That* for details," said Voltaire himself. "Posterity could not care less. They are the worms that ruin great books." If Louis XIV had asked for a lawyer to present his case to eternity, he could not have discovered a better choice. For the *Age* can never be dismissed as the work of a toady. The king's faults are given all the attention they deserve, beginning with the senseless devastation of the Palatinate on two occasions by his armies, and ending with the revocation of the Edict of Nantes in 1685. This last mistake cost France a million solid Huguenots who went into exile in England, Holland, and Prussia where their talents were fully appreciated. Louis the warrior is not revered, although his joy on learning that Charles II of Spain left his realm to Louis' grandson, the Duc d'Anjou, is made plain. At this news Louis plunged into the War of the Spanish Succession, the last and most disastrous of his military adventures.

Louis could be vain, as Voltaire realized. When the Spanish ambassador to the Court of Saint James presumed to take precedence over the French ambassador, he threatened war and Madrid was humbled. Yet there was a limit to the king's vanity. When the French Academy proposed to discuss which of his virtues was the most remarkable, he canceled all such talk at once.

"He did not accomplish all that he could," Voltaire pointed out, "because he was a man. But since he was a great man, he accomplished more than anyone else." As a man, he had his love affairs. These, quite properly, are treated like the love affairs of Jupiter. He did not die like an ordinary mortal. "I'd thought it would be more difficult to die," he told those at his bedside. "Why are you weeping? Did you imagine that I was immortal?"

But he was immortal, Voltaire believed. For he made French the language of Europe and saw to it that French civilization was supreme. In this area no fault could be found: the development of French architecture, painting, sculpture, and music was astonishing. We might quibble in our time over the patronage of music, since he neglected the genius of Marc-Antoine Charpentier in favor of the talent of Lully, but then music was of slight interest to Voltaire. He was on surer grounds when treating the other arts and surest of all when it came to literature.

Although Louis arrived too late to be of much assistance to Corneille, he did his best to encourage Molière and Racine, honoring the latter for an ode he wrote at eighteen. "Corneille won his own reputation," Voltaire admitted, "but Louis XIV, Sophocles, and Euripides contributed to the creation of Racine," who was even invited to join the select company at the château of Marly. The asocial LaFontaine was not taken up at court—which was just as well, since he enjoyed solitude—but Boileau was given the right to differ with the king in the matter of poetry. He's quite right," said Louis. "He's a better authority than I." As for La Bruyère, he was admitted to the Academy even if his *Caractères* were not calculated to win friends. And even Fénelon, too whimsical for the taste of the court, was entrusted with the education of Louis' grandson, the Duc de Bourgogne.

With the exception of Pascal, whom Voltaire never could digest, the great writers of the age are discussed with disarming equanimity: Voltaire intended they should be the models of the next century.

Would the irreverent Voltaire have been made welcome in such a setting? The question is never raised. Nor is there a word about the faith of Louis, a topic of slight interest to the author. He did however investigate this aspect; in his notebooks he jotted down the comment of His Majesty on the defeat at Ramillies in 1706. "How could God have forgotten," Louis asked, "all the things I did for Him?"

The *Age of Louis XIV*, no matter what its merits, was not well received in the Paris of Louis XV, who may have dreaded the comparison that could be made between his taste and that of his great-grandfather. The book was reprinted in Leipzig, Dresden, and Geneva but only surreptitiously in France. Official opinion of Voltaire was such that he was not allowed to return to Paris until 1778, the year of his death.

In Berlin Voltaire was exasperated by the behavior of Laurent Angliviel de La Beaumelle, whose one aim was to discredit this work. "I know very well," cried Voltaire, "that enjoying a literary career means fighting one war after another, but really, I didn't expect this man's invasion."

If La Beaumelle had been merely impertinent, he might have been overlooked, but he was a spiteful enemy. Having got his hands on the correspondence of Madame de Maintenon, the mistress and finally the wife of Louis XIV, he refused to allow a glimpse of his haul, and his unauthorized edition of the *Age* was throbbing not only with historical errors of major importance but also with major insults. "There are better poets than Voltaire," he claimed, "but no poet has been better paid. The King of Prussia overwhelms men of letters with his generosity, for the very same reason that German princes overwhelm their dwarfs and buffoons."

La Beaumelle also wormed himself into the confidence of Maupertuis, then engaged in a quarrel with the mathematician Samuel König over the authenticity of certain letters of Leibnitz. Voltaire believed, correctly, that König was telling the truth. He may have been amused at the outset by the antics of Maupertuis. But when he learned that the President of the Berlin Academy was planning to perforate the center of the earth, there to dissect the brain of a Patagonian in order to investigate the nature of the soul, Voltaire became alarmed. Nor was he reassured by Maupertuis' advice that a different doctor be consulted for every ailment, and no physician paid for anything less than a complete cure. Finally, when Maupertuis decided that the bodies of the sick should be covered with pitch to prevent all perspiration, Voltaire could not resist the temptation of attacking him in print.

In November 1752 he published *La Diatribe du Docteur Akakia*, a pamphlet in which Maupertuis' oddities were treated with less than respect. An earlier pamphlet, defending König, had been answered by Frederick himself, who was not delighted by this challenge to the dignity of the president of his Academy. "Your effrontery amazes me," wrote Frederick to Voltaire. "You can't make me believe that black is white." He had *Akakia* burned in public and the ashes delivered to Maupertuis, telling him that "I've given him such a dressing down that I don't think he'll cause any more trouble, and I know that cowardly soul of his without a single honorable instinct. I made it quite plain to him that my house should be a sanctuary and not a hideout for thieves, where criminals distill their poisons."

But this is not the whole story. One minute Frederick was thinking of the insult to his own prestige, another he was laughing out loud at Voltaire's prose—this on the very day he set *Akakia* on fire in the author's presence. Then, on December 27 he sent Voltaire a statement he was required to sign, in which he promised to write against no one, neither the French government, nor other sovereigns, nor against distinguished men of letters entitled to respect. Voltaire agreed to all this, but on the eighteenth had already written Madame Denis that the orange was being squeezed. "We must now think about saving the skin . . . For my own use," he added, "I am drawing up a small dictionary for corresponding with kings. *My friend* means *my slave. My dear friend* means that *I couldn't care less.* By *I'll make you happy* you must understand that *I'll put up with you as long as I need you. Have dinner with me this evening* signifies that *I'll subject you to ridicule this evening.* This is getting to be quite a big dictionary."

Copies of the *Diatribe* were circulating from hand to hand all over Berlin. In his fury Frederick had the pamphlet burned by the public executioner not too far from the house where Voltaire was living in the Taubenstrasse. "I'll bet you they are burning my doctor!" Voltaire cried to his secretary. He could look on the scene from his window.

By January 15, 1753, he was telling Madame Denis that he had sent back to the Solomon of the North the sheepbell and that other trinket she shamed him for accepting. This was a reference to his key as chamberlain and the order of *Pour le Mérite.*

> *Je les reçus avec tendresse,*
> *Je vous les rends avec douleur;*
> *C'est ainsi qu'un amant, dans son extrême ardeur,*
> *Rend le portrait de sa maîtresse.*

[*I received them with tenderness,/I give them back to you with sorrow;/Thus a lover, in his greatest passion,/Returns the portrait of his mistress.*]

wrote Voltaire at half past three in the afternoon of New Year's Day. But inside of half an hour, the grand factotum Federsdorff was on hand giving the "trinkets" back. Frederick wrote, Voltaire went on to his niece, "he'd rather have me on hand than Maupertuis. One thing is certain, I can't stand living with either one of them."

On January 15 Frederick was trying to make a benevolent impression. "The King has held his consistory," he informed Voltaire, "and in this consistory the issue was raised whether your case was a mortal or a venial sin. To tell you the truth, the doctors have judged it was a very mortal sin, as proved by your constant falling from grace. But nevertheless, by the plenitude of Beelzebub's grace, which resides in His Majesty, he thinks he may be able to absolve you, if not wholly at least partially . . . Since in Satan's realm, the utmost deference is paid to genius, I believe that your faults might be forgiven."

On January 30 Voltaire was invited back to Potsdam to occupy his usual apartment. This invitation he declined. His erysipelas, complicated by an attack of dysentery, made that impossible. Quinine was immediately forthcoming from the royal palace, but he insisted he could properly recover only by taking the waters at Plombières. The waters at Glatz would do just as well, came the word from Frederick. "It was not necessary," he wrote Voltaire on March 16, "for you to use Plombières as a pretext. You may leave me whenever you want; but before you leave, you must surrender your contract, your key, your cross [meaning *Pour le Mérite*], and the volume of poetry I left in your hands."

He did spend another week in Postdam as Frederick's guest. Then, on the morning of March 26, he came up just as the king was reviewing his troops. "Sire," the king was told, "here is Monsieur de Voltaire come to receive Your Majesty's orders." "Well," Voltaire was asked, "you really want to leave?" "Sire," came the answer, "urgent business and especially my health leave me no alternative." "I wish you a safe trip," said Frederick.

But not too safe. For Voltaire forgot to return his contract, his chamberlain's key, and the order of *Pour le Mérite*, not to mention the poems. Stopping first in Leipzig, then in Gotha and Cassel, he reached Frankfurt on May 29, where Madame Denis joined him a few days later. She had prudently refused Frederick's offer of a pension of four thousand francs as her uncle's house-keeper in Potsdam. With this decision Voltaire could find no fault. "This country is not made for you," he told her.

In Frankfurt he discovered that he was not yet free of Frederick, who seemed to be almost as nervous as Maupertuis where Voltaire was concerned. Maupertuis had informed Voltaire that "if you plan to attack me, as you have already attacked me, by damaging my character, I must tell you that, instead of answering you in writing, my health is good enough for me to seek you out wherever you are, and to exact my complete revenge."

Voltaire was no sooner installed at the Golden Lion Inn than Baron Franz von Freytag, Frederick's agent in Frankfurt, knocked on his door, accompanied by his faithful Schmid. Freytag had been banished from Dresden after serving a sentence at hard labor, but this, as Voltaire did not need to be told, was really a qualification, since Frederick was fond of hiring men who worked for no salary, only what they could steal from travelers. As for Schmid, he had been fined for counterfeiting, but this did him no harm either. In the supposed Free City of Frankfurt, the king of Prussia could not care less who represented him or what damage was done the principles of international law.

Voltaire could not leave town, he was directed by Freytag and Schmid, until he "returned the precious objects belonging to His Majesty." "Alas," wrote Voltaire in his account of the incident, "I am not carrying anything away from that country, not even the slightest regrets. What are the jewels of the crown of Brandenburg that you demand?" In his illiterate French Freytag explained that he must have the "poéshie" of the king his most gracious master. "Oh," Voltaire countered, "I'll gladly return his prose and poetry, although, after all, my rights are involved. He made me a present of a beautiful book printed at his expense. Unfortunately, this copy is in Leipzig with my other belongings."

Upon which Freytag, who did not forget to ask for the chamberlain's key and *Pour le Mérite*, proposed that Voltaire remain in Frankfurt until Frederick was satisfied. Freytag then signed a paper offering to release his victim once the trunk from Leipzig came with the manuscript of the royal poems.

On the seventeeth of June the trunk with the "poéshie" was on hand, and was surrendered. Since all of the stipulations had been met, Voltaire thought he might be a free man. This was not to be. A dozen soldiers turned up, dragging Voltaire, his secretary, and Madame Denis to what appeared to be the lowest inn in town. Four soldiers were quartered in Voltaire's room, another four, armed with bayonets, watched over Madame Denis, and still another four were stationed in a garret as a further guard on the prisoners.

Voltaire had applied for assistance from the emperor of Austria, but none was forthcoming, "My niece," he was careful to point out, "was bearing a passport of the King of France, and besides, she had never corrected the verses of the King of Prussia." He tried to run away, once he met Frederick's apparent demands, but to no use. His cash on hand was stolen, and he was presented with a bill for twelve days of detention under guard.

Finally on July 2, 1753, he left Frankfurt for Mainz, and Madame Denis was allowed to make her way to Paris. "Once this business with the Ostrogoths and Vandals was over, I embraced my hosts," he wrote, "and thanked them for their sweet reception."

But let no one believe that Voltaire bore a lasting grudge against Frederick the Great. He *had* enjoyed his stay with the Solomon of the North: he had come to know, intimately, a powerful man.

The two would resume their curious correspondence. Voltaire was not one to lose his sense of humor. "The King of Prussia has just written me a friendly letter," he advised the Duc de Richelieu in the winter of 1757. "Things must be going badly for him."

5

THOSE GUILTY CHAIRS

Frederick could always be disagreeable. This trait was apparent to the Marquis d'Argenson, once Voltaire's schoolmate and later the Secretary of Foreign Affairs. Observed d'Argenson in his memoirs: "They have refused to grant the poet Voltaire permission to return to France. They are planning by this maneuver to please the King of Prussia, while managing to displease him in more important matters."

But Frederick was never a menace. This privilege fell to Jean-Jacques Rousseau, the specialist in guilt who claimed that a sense of shame was the badge of virtue: *Criminals have no shame.* For Voltaire, who knew that guilt was nothing but unnecessary baggage, here was the one man who could rob him of his peace of mind. He was the very symbol of the romantic movement, exulting in sentiment, reveling in the beauties of nature and preaching the joys of lascivious innocence. These were so many opportunities that Voltaire had chosen to ignore. And the fact that Rousseau was the master of a passionate prose that challenged the classic perfection of the seventeenth century did not make him any more attractive.

Nor was he delighted to recognize that this intruder on the literary scene possessed the unholy gift of calling attention to himself. This gift was evident in 1750, when the thirty-eight-year-old Rousseau succeeded in slicing the century in half by persuading the French that the incredible art of their cabinetmakers was a sinful thing: sitting in the most beautiful chairs the world had ever seen, they were sitting in guilty chairs.*

Such was the revelation that came to Rousseau while trudging from Paris to Vincennes to call on his friend Denis Diderot, who happened to be in prison for the moment. The Academy of Dijon, he noticed in the latest *Mercure de France*, was offering a prize for the best essay on the subject: *Has the revival of the sciences and the arts contributed to the corruption or the purification of our morals?* "I glimpsed another universe and became a different man," Rousseau recalled. "By the time I reached Vincennes I was trembling, I was delirious. Diderot was aware of this. I told him the cause. He encouraged me to express my ideas and compete for the prize. I did so, and from that moment I was lost. All the rest of my life and all my misfortunes were the inevitable result of this aberration."

He dared, he argued in this prize-winning work, to defend the cause of virtue. "A vile and deceitful uniformity is prevalent: we no longer presume to be what we are." Sparta, he admitted, would always be an inspiration. As for Athens, we owe to her those surprising achievements that serve as models in corrupt times. "Tell us," he went on, "O famous Arouet, how many manly beauties have you sacrificed to our false delicacy? . . . We have plenty of physicists, geometricians, chemists, astronomers, poets, musicians, and painters, but we no longer have any citizens, or if some are still with us, scattered in the desolate countryside, they are dying, miserable paupers."

Although he did not denounce in so many words the marvels of cabinetmakers the like of the Migeons, the Cressons, the Tilliards, the Van Risen Burghs, and the others who followed after André-Charles Boulle, it was obvious that they were pernicious, catering to luxury like all the great architects, painters, and sculptors, "A taste for luxury," he made plain, "always occurs when a taste for literature develops." This was sad. So was the condition of all artists, who live only to be praised.

The time had come for a new morality, Rousseau implied.

---

*Was this his own idea? The malicious German Friedrich Melchior Grimm thought not: It *became* his idea when he had to defend it.

Faithful to this mission, he completed in 1754 his important essay on the origins of inequality. "The first man to put up a fence around his land, say *this is mine* and find people so simple-minded as to believe him, was the real originator of society," he declared. "How many crimes, how many wars, how much misery, and how much horror might have been spared mankind, if someone, tearing up the fence posts or filling up the ditches, had cried out to his fellows: *Stop listening to that impostor!*"

Voltaire, whose reverence for private property does not need to be underlined, was not too grateful for this essay. "I have received," he wrote him, "your new book against the human race . . . No one has ever taken more trouble to turn us all into fools. Anyone who reads your book will want to crawl on all fours. However, I gave up that habit more than sixty years ago, and unfortunately can't start over again." Then, obviously referring to his strictures on the arts and sciences, he added: "I agree with you that literature and science have sometimes caused a great deal of trouble." Yet, he pointed out, the tragedy of *Le Cid* was not responsible for the civil war that greeted the youth of Louis XIV.

But Rousseau was incorrigible. "When I offered you this sketch of my sad daydreams, I had no idea of sending you a present worthy of you, but only thought of fulfilling a duty and paying the homage we all owe you, our leader . . . So don't try to fall down on all fours," he pleaded. "No one could be less successful than you in performing that act . . . A taste for letters and the arts comes about as the result of a void in a nation, a void that can only be increased. As for me, if I had followed my first inclination and read nothing and written nothing, I should doubtless have been a happier man . . . The more people criticize you, the more you will be admired."

They had first recognized each other under more pleasant circumstances. Toward the end of 1745 Rousseau was moved to apologize for the changes he was making in Voltaire's text for Rameau's *Princesse de Navarre,* an entertainment planned for the wedding of the Dauphin to the Infanta of Spain. "For fifteen years," wrote Rousseau to Voltaire, "I have been trying to make myself worthy of the kindness you bestow on young artists in whom you discover some talent." He was only making the changes, he said, to please the Duc de Richelieu. Voltaire made a gracious reply, congratulating him on his claim to be a composer as well as a poet. "You unite two talents which have always been separated until this moment. These are two good reasons for me to esteem you and try to be your friend. I am only sorry for you that you must waste these two talents of yours on a work which is not really worthy of you."

At first glance Rousseau must have seemed, as he did to many people, a professional failure. That was the disguise that this son of an improvident Geneva clockmaker assumed again and again. He was also too fond of imploring mercy and forgiveness to pass for a second as a victorious lover, yet he was to haunt woman after woman, beginning with his "Mama," Madame de Warens, to whom he was introduced at sixteen by a curé who hoped to make a convert of this runaway boy. Madame de Warens, then twenty-eight, took him into her household at Annecy in Savoy; thirty-two days later he was received into the Roman Church. He was to remain a Roman for twenty-six years, but his enjoyment of Mama meant more to him. "Two or three times," he confessed, "gathering her into my arms, I drenched her breasts with my tears. It was as if I had committed incest." Not exactly. As he described his love for her, it was not love at all, but something far more possessive, having nothing to do with the senses, with sexuality, or with their age. It was his self and her self, it was a devotion that would last as long as they lived. "I would embrace her in her bed when she was still half asleep, and that embrace, in its very innocence, possessed a charm divorced from all voluptuousness."

He could and did live without her. Passing himself off as a professional musician long before he was competent, he wandered off to Lyons, to Lausanne, and to Neuchâtel. Eventually he served nearly a year as secretary to the French ambassador in Venice. He quarreled with him as he did with so many other people and by 1741 was in Paris copying music to earn his living and trying his hand as a composer. In the fall of 1752 his opera *The Village Soothsayer* was performed before Louis XV at Fontainebleau. The King, who did his best to sing the air "J'ai perdu mon serviteur," was charmed, but Rousseau was difficult, too shy

Jean-Antoine Houdon, *Voltaire*. Musée de Versailles.

Photograph, Roger-Viollet

Marianne Loir, *Portrait de la Marquise du Châtelet.* 102 × 80 cm. Musée de Beaux-Arts, Bordeaux.

Château de Cirey.   Photograph by Wayne Andrews

Les Délices (Geneva).   Photograph by Wayne Andrews

Château de Ferney.   Photograph by Wayne Andrews

Church at Ferney.   Photograph by Wayne Andrews

Jean-Antoine Houdon, *Jean-Jacques Rousseau.* Staatliches Museum, Schwerin. Courtesy of F. de Noble, publisher of Louis Réau, *Houdin: Sa Vie et Son Oeuvre,* Paris 1964.

Rephotographed by George Booth, Jr.

Jean-Antoine Houdon, *Seated Figure of Voltaire* (1778). Plaster, 8⅜".
Walters Art Gallery, Baltimore.

Charles Nicholas Cochin, *Voltaire and [His Niece] Madame Denis.*
Crayon on paper, 4½″ × 6½″. Courtesy of The New-York Historical
Society, New York City.

J. G. Glume, *Frederick the Great*. Charlottenburg Museum, Berlin.
Photograph, Atelier Jörg P. Anders

85

Samuel Freeman, *Madame du Deffand*. Engraving after a water color of
Carmontelle, formerly at Strawberry Hill. Courtesy of the Lewis Walpole
Library, Farmington, Connecticut.

to submit to an interview. So he lost the pension due him, although he did accept a hundred louis and an additional fifty from Madame de Pompadour, who assumed the role of Colin when the opera was staged at her château of Bellevue. "I lost, it is true, that pension," said Rousseau, "but I also freed myself of the yoke I should have borne. Farewell to truth, freedom, and courage! How could I ever speak again of independence?"

He was singularly independent of the five children supplied by his mistress, the seamstress Thérèse Levasseur. "I believe," he wrote, "that I acted the part of a citizen and a father. I should like to have been supported and educated as they were." All five were surrendered to the care of a foundling home. In the meantime *The Village Soothsayer* had made him the fashion, and we have his word for it that no one in Paris was more sought after than he.

Taken up by Louise Dupin, the daughter of the omnipotent financier Samuel Bernard, he was also encouraged by the Duchesse de Boufflers (later married to the Marèchal-Duc de Luxembourg). He was even given the liberty of a house of his own on the Luxembourg estate at Montmorency. Another important friend was Louise de la Live d'Epinay, whose sister-in-law the Comtesse d'Houdetot shared for a time her affections between Rousseau and Saint-Lambert, the former lover of Madame du Châtelet.

So he could count on connections, especially in the winter of 1761, when his novel *La Nouvelle Héloise* went on sale in Paris. The first page could not have been improved. "No chaste girl has ever read a novel," he began. "And the title I have given mine is so definite that anyone opening the book should know what to expect. Any girl who, in spite of the title, dares to read a single page, is lost. But she must not blame her fall upon this book. The evil was already done. And since she has started, she might as well finish: she no longer runs any risk."

According to Rousseau, a copy was delivered to the Princesse de Talmont (that was not her real name, but no matter) the day of the ball at the Opera. After supper she got dressed to go, and to pass the time began reading the new novel. At midnight she called for her carriage and kept on reading. When they came to tell her the carriage was ready, she did not reply. Her servants, noticing that she had forgotten everything except the book, warned her that it was now two in the morning. "There's no hurry," she said and kept on reading. A little later she realized that her watch had stopped and rang to ask what time it was. They told her it was four o'clock. "If that's the case," she answered, "it's too late to go to the ball. Send my horses back to the stable." She then undressed and spent the rest of the night reading.

What she was reading was not so much an eighteenth-century novel as an advertisement of the wonders of the century to come. The guilty love of Julie d'Etange for her tutor Saint-Preux is a passionate affair, and passion had been neglected in the world that Voltaire so coolly commanded. Nor had the beauties of nature been studied with the attention here displayed. Wild flowers were what Rousseau preferred. In the secret garden of Julie, "the fountain plays only for strangers, the brook plays *for us.*"

Voltaire might have singled out the remarkable last chapters, in which Julie's husband invites Saint-Preux to live with them, celebrating her perfect chastity. But what caught Voltaire's eye was the "acrid kisses" exchanged between Julie and Saint-Preux. Posing as a certain Marquis de Ximénès (who generously allowed the use of his name, having purloined not so long before one of the master's manuscripts) Voltaire wrote four letters to himself about this inexcusable novel.

Voltaire noticed that the "blooming complexion" of Julie "outrages" her lover. Whereupon she gives him a very long and very "acrid" kiss. He does complain about this, and the next day gets her with child. As for his adventures in a Paris brothel, they are so many sacrifices on the altar of her divinity, even though he does come down with the smallpox. Did all this add up to a novel? Voltaire said no. "A novel, no matter how frivolous, demands genius . . . and the skill to invent a plot. Jean-Jacques' only desire was to teach something to our nation." On reflection, Voltaire decided that the book should have been written in a brothel.

But even before he turned the first page, he was positive that Rousseau had gone "completely insane." Nor was he reconciled by the publication the following year of *Du Contrat Social* and

Emile, both of which were burned by the authorities in Geneva. The very notion of the quasi-divine General Will, the core of Rousseau's political economy, was distasteful to one accustomed to intimacy with the autocratic Frederick the Great. Moreover, the future of Russia as sketched in the former tract was found to be an absurd invention. "The Russian Empire," ran the argument, "will attempt to subjugate Europe and will be subjugated itself. The Tartars, their neighbors, or their subjects, will become their masters and ours. This revolution appears to be inevitable. All the kings of Europe are co-operating to speed this development on its way." At this news, Voltaire lost his patience. "The court at Petersburg," he warned, "will take us for so many astrologers if it learns that one of our apprentice-watchmakers has set the hour on which the Russian Empire will be destroyed . . . They've burned this book here. Burning it must have been almost as boring as writing it."

When it came to *Emile*, Rousseau obviously had no right to lecture parents on the art of bringing up children. "May the Lord preserve your Most Serene Highness from the fate of having one of your sons educated by that madman Jean-Jacques Rousseau," he was telling the Duchess of Saxe-Gotha in the summer of 1762. "No one can educate anyone else who hasn't received a good education himself."

However, something could be said in favor of *Emile*. One unexpected character in this treatise was the vicar from Savoy who, once his misspent youth was revealed, got into trouble with his bishop. This vicar could hardly be considered a blessing to the Roman Church. He had been told he must believe everything; this made it impossible for him to believe anything. So he shut up all the books in his library and placed his faith in the one book open to every man: the book of nature. All this could be construed as an attack on Christianity, and there were moments when Voltaire was ready to forgive everything, or almost everything. Confiding in Madame du Deffand, he wrote: "If ever I said a word about Rousseau except in favor of the *Vicaire Savoyard* for which he was condemned, I should be looked upon as the most miserable of men. In these cruel times when we should respect his misfortune and appreciate his genius, I have not wanted to read a single one of the attacks upon him." Indeed, when he dwelled on the thought that the author of the *Vicaire* might be persecuted, he broke into tears. "Let him come to me!" he cried. "Let him come to me. I'll receive him with open arms . . . I'll treat him like my own son."

This mood did not last for long, nor did the two men cease from tormenting each other.

Rousseau, of course, was not the only topic that concerned Voltaire since the day he slipped out of Frankfurt and Madame Denis went on her way to Paris. The rumor has been spread, and there seems no reason to doubt it, that Madame Denis was not above blackmailing her uncle. At least she hinted, falsely, that she was pregnant. The matter must have been on her lover's mind as he wandered through the Germanies while in search of a permanent home. He was tempted to consider the château of Haroué in Lorraine, but this quite successful effort by the great Germain Boffrand was an expensive proposition, and luxury, as we well know, was always something for other people to enjoy, not Voltaire.

At last, in January 1755, after dallying in Mainz, Manheim, Schwetzingen, Württemberg, and Strasbourg, and obtaining the special dispensation required of a Roman Catholic intending to live in the city of Geneva, he bought up the château of Saint-Jean on the outskirts of town, renaming it Les Délices. Although the château had once belonged to the son of the Prince de Gotha, this was no princely residence. Here was a conventional house of no architectural distinction, but a convenient place in which to stage his own plays. The idea that he might pollute the morals of the city by having his own theater had immediately occurred to the authorities, who wondered what he might not do with his niece at his side.

Wrote the pastor Jean-Jacob Vernet: "The only thing (I am coming right out with this, since you honor me by calling me your friend) which has somewhat disturbed the general satisfaction of welcoming a man as celebrated as you are, is the idea which your youthful writings have given the public about your feelings on the very basis of religion."

About this time the Genevan bookseller François Grasset had the audacity to place on the market a few copies of *La Pucelle*.

"This manuscript is not mine," Voltaire complained when the book was burned by the authorities. "It is an infamous rhapsody, as dull and coarse as it is indecent." He blamed Frederick the Great for its publication, accusing him of hoping that he would thus be obliged to seek asylum once again in Postdam. He also had Grasset arrested, jailed, and exiled from Geneva. In the meantime he went ahead staging his plays, importing one of his favorite actors, LeKain, to be sure of an audience. When the audience appeared and Genevans grew anxious, he set up still another stage at Monriond, his house at Lausanne.

Switzerland was beginning to be a trial. Finally, to be sure of his independence, he made himself in October 1758 the owner of the château of Ferney in France, just across the Genevan border. This was to be his permanent address; he got rid of Les Délices by the beginning of 1765. Like Les Délices, Ferney was devoid of all architectural interest, even after his architect Léonard Racle made a few additions.* The interior was left in Madame Denis' hands. "My uncle," she said, "knows nothing about furnishing a living-room." He also acquired a life interest in the immediately adjacent comté de Tournay. Here he was safe from feudal dues and could pose as the lord of the manor. Which did not prevent him in the years to come from indulging in a ferocious quarrel with his landlord, the président de Brosses.

Banned he might be from Paris, but he did not neglect for a second the new *Encyclopédie* launched in 1751 by Denis Diderot and Jean d'Alembert. Although the editors ostensibly modeled their publication after *Chambers' Encyclopedia* of 1728, their far from invisible aim was not to supply so much information on so many topics but to discredit Christianity. "You and Diderot," Voltaire had written d'Alembert from Berlin in the fall of 1752, "are doing a work that will be the glory of France and the shame of those who have persecuted you. There are scribblers aplenty in Paris, but I recognize as eloquent philosophers only the two of you." Of course he had to contribute himself; of course he had to drown the editors with compliments. "As long as I have a breath of life in me, I shall place myself at the call of you illustrious

*Voltaire considered that an architect was not really necessary. "I built my château without consulting anyone," he bragged.

authors. I shall be highly honored to make my contribution, feeble though it may be, to the greatest and most beautiful monument to the nation and to literature," he wrote in 1755.

At the same time he did not need to be told that many of the articles were too long and that the ponderous volumes of the *Encyclopédie* were best read on a lectern. He grew fond of his own *Dictionnaire Philosophique*. "Evil people have attributed it to me," he told Madame du Deffand. "What an atrocious calumny! . . . I am sorry that such a dangerous book is so easy to get hold of . . . I am assured that your edition is more ample and more insolent than all the others. I haven't seen it. You may judge of it and condemn it if there is anything amiss. But to my shame I must admit that in general I like short chapters that don't tire the mind."

So far as we know, Voltaire and Diderot never met face to face. This was fortunate, for the distance between a professional deist and a professional atheist would have been immediately apparent.

Diderot was an atheist. Since atheists come in all sizes, the point must be made that he was never a desperate poet on the order of Nietzsche. He would never cry out, as did Nietzsche, that the time had come to *correct the future and redeem the past*. In Diderot's eyes God was a maniac misanthropist whose mission was to infatuate mankind. "Morality," he proclaimed, "can exist without religion, and religion can exist, and often does, with immorality." As for theologians, they were sinister. Wrote Diderot: "Lost in an immense forest at night, I have only a little light to show me the way. Along comes a stranger who says to me 'Friend, blow out your candle the better to find your way.' This stranger is a theologian." Simple solutions were always preferred. "Posterity is always just," he claimed, forgetting that posterity may be a fallible guide. His benefactress Catherine the Great came close to understanding him when she reported that he was a hundred years old in some respects, but only ten years old in others.

For this comfortable man, almost any problem could be solved once God was eliminated. He and his likeminded friends—one thinks of Helvétius, author of the tract *De l'Esprit*, and of Baron Holbach, author of *Le Système Social*—were evidently highly pleased by the state of bliss in which they, as professional atheists, found themselves. To bring Diderot and his circle back to life, we must imagine the moment when Hume arrived from England to inspect the Paris scene and turned up at Holbach's table. When Hume ventured to tell his host that he didn't believe in atheists, never having met one, Holbach asked him to count all the guests. There were eighteen. "I'll have no trouble in pointing out fifteen to you," he was told. "The other three haven't yet made up their minds."

Diderot was an industrious man, which did him no harm at all when he faced the drudgery of managing the *Encyclopédie*. And since he was not famous for his wit, he was spared the suspicion so often attached to Voltaire.

Jesuit-trained, Diderot disagreed so completely with his teachers that he determined all mystery should be removed not only from religion but from sex as well. So, to instruct his daughter in the facts of life, he obliged her to study wax anatomical models. The pornography for which he was so famous at the time makes for joyless reading in the twentieth century. Neither *Les Bijoux Indiscrets* nor *La Religieuse*, this last an exposé of lesbianism in a nunnery, would lead anyone astray. Ever in earnest, he could not describe the world of a man blind at birth, as he did in his *Lettre sur les Aveugles*, without pointing out that the blind Englishman Sanderson remained unconvinced of the existence of God. For this comment, seized upon by the diligent censors of Louis XV, he spent a few months in the prison of Vincennes, where Rousseau came to visit him.

Although he was not aware of the existence of art until he was thirty-seven, he made himself into an art critic at the urging of his German friend Friedrich Melchior Grimm. The sculptor Pigalle, then at work on his monument to the Maréchal de Saxe, seems to have been surprised by this sudden interest in the arts. Should he be allowed to observe a model in the nude? "Promise me," said Pigalle, "that you won't be afraid of a beautiful woman without a stitch of clothing on." In Diderot's eyes the frank sensuality of Boucher was immoral. He was an expert, he decided, in debauchery. Besides, his coloring was false, and connoisseurs of the grand, antique, and severe taste should not pay any attention to his work.

Diderot's hero was Greuze. When he came upon his *Filial Piety* in the Salon of 1763, he declared: "This is just what I like: it is moral painting. Come now! Hasn't the brush been dedicated long enough to debauchery and vice? Shouldn't we be satisfied to watch the brush compete with dramatic poetry in moving our souls, in teaching us, in correcting us, and in inviting us to do good works? Chin up, my friend Greuze! Give us a moral message in painting and keep on doing just that." He was sounding the keynote of what ultimately became the doctrine of social realism in Nazi Germany and Communist Russia. It is true that he did encourage his friend Falconet to create the heroic statue of Peter the Great in Saint Petersburg. At the time Falconet, who had Jansenist tendencies, may have been tired of turning out so many girlies for the Sèvres pottery works.

Diderot and his circle were fond of describing themselves as *philosophes*. "Philosophers" would be the literal translation, but "intellectuals," while less pretentious, quite conveys their idea of their rank in society. In polite society they occasionally ran into difficulties, although Madame de Pompadour put in a good word for the *Encyclopèdie* at Versailles. She was sorry that it was suppressed for a time by the censors, for she found it a useful reference work. It was the only place she could read up on the origin of the rouge she put on her cheeks.

The keepers of the greater salons of Paris were more difficult. Diderot and his friends were rarely seen in the townhouse of the Prince de Conti, whose marvelous rococo setting was immortalized, with Mozart at the keyboard, in the famous painting of Ollivier. Nor were they tolerated at the home of Madame Geoffrin. She would not allow Diderot to cross her threshold, although she did consent to see him at Holbach's. According to one of her friends, "she did not want a republic to be created in her house of which she would be the slave." As for Madame du Deffand, she found the group impossible and never forgave d'Alembert for robbing her of her companion Julie de Lespinasse.

Like Julie de Lespinasse, d'Alembert was illegitimate. Abandoned as a baby on the steps of the church of Saint-Jean Lerond, he was the son of Madame de Tencin—sister of the cardinal of Lyons—and the Chevalier Destouches. The father, who left him

an annuity of twelve thousand pounds but refused to acknowledge him, once made the mistake of introducing the boy to his
mother. "You must confess," Destouches told her, "that it would
have been a shame if this child had been forsaken." "Let me get
out of here," came the answer from Madame de Tencin, "for I can
see that I don't belong here."

D'Alembert, who nursed an undying hatred for Madame du
Deffand—"that dreadful old whore" as he called her—was nothing if not a mathematician. "Mathematics have been my mistress," he claimed, and the Jansenist education he received gave
him no sympathy for the Roman Catholic Church. He was first
and foremost a geometrician, although Voltaire had respect for
his prose. "You are," he told him, "the only writer who never
forgets to come right to the point. I think you are the first of our
century." He had his best interest at heart when he warned him
not to bring the *Encyclopédie* to Berlin. There were censors in
Paris, Voltaire allowed, but reminded d'Alembert from Sans Souci
that "there is a prodigious number of bayonets here and very few
books."

If given the chance, thought Voltaire, what might not d'Alembert do to undermine the Calvinist creed in Geneva? When the
time came for d'Alembert to write the article on Geneva for the
Encyclopédie, he put himself out to be of service. And the article,
seemingly flattering to the local clergy, was everything that Voltaire could have wished for. "The clergy," d'Alembert explained,
"have exemplary morals. But you must not believe that they all
think alike when it comes to what are regarded as the most
important truths of religion. Many of the clergy no longer believe
in the divinity of Jesus Christ . . . In a word, several pastors in
Geneva have no other religion than pure socinianism." He went
on to say that the music was in bad taste in the Protestant temples,
and quoted Voltaire's saying that Calvin had "an atrocious
soul."

Rousseau had yet to be heard from. His *Lettre à d'Alembert sur
les Spectacles* put an end, as he doubtless intended, to his friendship with Diderot and made any reconciliation with Voltaire
impossible. "It is neither advantageous nor attractive for me to
attack Monsieur d'Alembert," Rousseau began. "I esteem him as

a person; I admire his talents." Not too deeply. "You say that several pastors in Geneva are pure socinians. I dare to ask you: how did you find this out?" With this, Rousseau proclaimed himself the friend of any peaceful religion.

It was evident that the stage was Rousseau's real enemy, and quite possibly his diatribe, released in March 1758, had some ultimate influence. At least no plays were performed in Geneva from 1768, when the new theater on the Place Neuve went up in flames, until 1782.

"The people have to have plays that will appeal to their inclinations," Rousseau decided, "but what is needed is plays that will moderate their inclinations . . . Comedies are good for good people, but bad for bad people." From this he went on to argue that ridicule has always been the favorite weapon of vice . . . Even the plays of Molière were really nothing but an education in vice and bad morals. And Molière had gone to the greatest trouble to make fun of the virtues of kindness and simplicity.

Actors were particularly reprehensible. In fact, forbidding a comedian to be vicious was a little like forbidding a man to fall sick. Tragedies might be tolerated, he notified Voltaire, comedies never. Once an auditorium is built for comedies, there is really no solution in sight. To allow the auditorium to stand is an error, tearing it down is another error. Once the first mistake has been made, we have only a choice of evils left us.

This argument may have been logical, but the logic did not please Voltaire. "They tell me," he complained to d'Alembert, "that he has carried sacrilege to the point of screaming against all comedies . . . They are simply crazy about plays in the country of Calvin. In three months' time, three new plays have been put on in Geneva itself, and of these three plays I've written only one."

The more he reflected on the outrageous remarks of Rousseau, the more kindly he felt to the men in charge of the *Encyclopédie*, no matter if their publication was a dull thing compared to his own dictionary. "You may complain as bitterly as you like about the encyclopedists," he was writing the Duc de Richelieu at the end of the Seven Years' War. "They are the dangerous people who made you lose Canada. Nothing could be more correct than to have them hanged, as you proposed in one of your gracious letters, but I should not like to be included in your verdict. I am not at all an encyclopedist. All that I am asking is not to have the rubbish that Rousseau is spreading all over this country attributed to me."

Worried sick by Rousseau, Voltaire was not his usual amusing self when he wrote d'Alembert that "I'd like to see you *écraser l'infâme* [freely translated, "crush that infamous thing," i.e., clerical superstition.] That's the important thing. We must reduce it to the state it is in over in England . . . That's the greatest service anyone can render mankind." Voltaire will forever be identified with this simple slogan, which is a shame, for the phrase was invented by Frederick on one of his exuberant days at Potsdam. "You could caress *l'infâme* with one hand and scratch it with the other," he wrote on May 18, 1759.

Voltaire was, it must be admitted, energetic when he discovered that Christianity was founded on Judaism. Page after page of his anti-Semitic slurs might be offered to prove his resentment of the Jewish influence on Christianity, but the pages might not be worth printing. He played no role in the history of anti-Semitism: anti-Semites have never enjoyed his irreverence for authority of any kind. He himself was puzzled when the Portuguese Jew Isaac de Pinto ventured to defend his race from the insults of the *Dictionaire Philosophique*. "Many people," wrote Voltaire, "cannot stomach either your laws or your books or your superstitions. They tell me that your nation has always done a great deal of harm to itself and to mankind. I could argue with you about the scientific knowledge that you attribute to the Jews of old, and prove to you that they knew nothing more than the French in the days of Chilperic."

All this while Rousseau took care that Rousseau was not forgotten. Although there is no room to enter into all the details of the history of Geneva in the eighteenth century, something must be said about the power and prestige of Le Petit Conseil and Le Conseil des Deux Cents, which managed to inhibit the democratic tendencies with which Rousseau considered himself affiliated. It was Le Petit Conseil that ordered the burning of *Emile* and *Du Contrat Social*, and their chief adviser was Attorney-General Jean-Robert Tronchin, who did, however, query the issuing of a warrant for Rousseau's arrest. Voltaire was well acquainted with

Jean-Robert Tronchin, and indeed with the entire Tronchin family. His physician was the surly Théodore Tronchin, his financial adviser was Robert Tronchin, and still another friend was the unsuccessful playwright François Tronchin, who made it possible for Voltaire the Catholic to settle at Les Délices. So it was no wonder that Rousseau blamed all of his troubles in his native city on the sinister influence of Voltaire.

"You talk to me about this Voltaire," Rousseau complained to a Genevan friend. "Why does the name of this buffoon soil your letters? The wretched man has corrupted my country. I should hate him more if I despised him less. For all his great talents, I see only his disgrace. He is dishonorable for the use he has made of his talents. Oh, people of Geneva! He is paying you off for the asylum you have given him. He did not know where else to go to do evil. You will be his last victim."

In his loathing of Voltaire Rousseau was not quite so lonely as he thought. The minister Jean-Jacob Vernet, the very man who had warned Voltaire not to misbehave within city limits, assured Dr. Théodore Tronchin that the author of the *Dictionnaire Philoso-phique* was up to no good. "You know," wrote Vernet, "how indiscreet he has been, how he has attacked and vilified religion, and blackened the name of our great reformer in chapters where I could point out ten or twelve notorious lies. How could you ask that I, in the position that I have the honor of occupying, having spent my life in defending religion, should hold my tongue and be civil?"

Voltaire would not hold his tongue concerning the Lisbon earthquake of November 1, 1755. Writing to Jean-Robert Tronchin less than a month later, he declared that "we shall be deeply embarrassed to guess how the laws of motion create such frightful disasters in the best of all possible worlds. A hundred thousand ants—our neighbors—have been suddenly crushed in an anthill, and half of them have perished . . . in the débris from which they cannot be extracted. What a sad game of chance is human life, the preachers will be telling us, especially if the palace of the Inquisi-tion is still standing. I flatter myself that the reverend inquisitors have been destroyed like everyone else. This should teach us not to persecute anyone, for while some damned rascals are putting a few fanatics to the stake, the earth has swallowed up everyone."

Although the earthquake was a moderate catastrophe in twentieth-century terms, a mere ten or fifteen thousand people having perished, Voltaire was not calm when he surveyed the damage done by the tidal wave and the flames that swept over the city. "I respect God," he wrote in his poem on the disaster, "but I love the universe." How could everything be for the best, he wondered, when thousands of children were crushed on the breasts of their mothers? Could Lisbon be accused of being a vicious city while Paris and London were surrendered to pleasure?

What he wrote was not a remarkable poem but it had a remarkable impact on Rousseau. "I have a difficult time," he told Voltaire, "in saving my sanity from the charms of your poetry, but it is only in order to make my admiration more worthy of your work that I try not to admire everything . . . All the complaints I have to offer have to do with your poem on the Lisbon disaster, since I was expecting results more worthy of the humanity which could have inspired you." Eventually, he reached the opinion that Voltaire, "while seeking to believe in God, really believes only in the devil, since the God he sets up is a dreadful being whose only pleasure lies in hurting us."

Dr. Théodore Tronchin might have agreed with this assessment of Voltaire's character. "What can one expect," Tronchin asked Rousseau, "from a man who is almost always in contradiction with himself, and whose heart has always been the dupe of his mind . . . He hasn't stolen his neighbor's wheat or taken his bull or his cow, but he has been guilty of other thefts in order to give himself a reputation and claim a superiority which any sane man would despise."

For all that, Rousseau insisted that Tronchin was Voltaire's ally. "You have your fill of glory," Rousseau reminded Voltaire in the summer of 1756, "and bored by the grandeurs of this world, you live a free man in the midst of prosperity. You have Tronchin for your doctor and your friend, but you see only evil on this earth. And I, forgotten by the world, tormented by a sickness for which there is no remedy, I take pleasure in meditating in my retreat, and find that all is for the best."

Not quite. When Attorney-General Jean-Robert Tronchin published, anonymously, his *Lettres Ecrites de la Campagne* defending the action of Le Petit Conseil in condemning *Emile* and *Du*

Contrat Social, Rousseau answered with his *Lettres Ecrites de la Montagne.* "Christianity," he had the presumption to declare, "making men righteous, moderate and lovers of the peace, is very advantageous to society at large, but it saps the energy of political life . . . It destroys the unity of our moral force . . . As for Calvin, he was doubtless a great man, but after all, he was a man, and what is worse a theologian." Rousseau added that the Calvinists of the day, at least the ministers, were not acquainted with their religion, and no longer loved it.

"When I arrived in this land," he concluded, "you would have said that the kingdom of France was at my heels. They burn my books in Geneva—that is to please France. They issue a warrant for my arrest—that is what France wants. They chase me out of the canton of Berne—that is what France requested."

Rousseau's troubles were momentarily overlooked, however, in January 1759 when Voltaire released *Candide,* the story that proved he despised optimism even more deeply than in the poem on Lisbon. On March 2 *Candide* was condemned by the authorities of Geneva and ordered destroyed. This could not have surprised the author. "Who are the lazy fools who attribute to me something called *Candide,* which is a schoolboy's joke?" he asked a pastor of his acquaintance. "I really have something else to do." Later on he would tell another friend: "The more I laugh over this thing, the sorrier I am that people assume I wrote it."

Candide may remain for all time the permanent advertisement of Voltaire's talent.

This is unfortunate. Respectfully mentioned in so many guides to French literature, and assigned so often as a text by unadventurous history professors, it conveys the rather dreadful impression that Voltaire was always as obvious as when relating the adventures of his simpleton hero.

There is, of course, an occasional page or two of the real Voltaire. He never could make sense of France's participation in the Seven Years' War that resulted in the loss of Canada and India. Canada, thought Voltaire, was nothing more than a few hundred acres of snow. This is set down in *Candide,* as is his opinion of the execution of the British Rear Admiral John Byng, court-martialed for his behavior in action against the French navy off Minorca. Ordered to relieve the island in May 1756, he withdrew inconclusively. Voltaire, who pitied Byng, got the French commander, the Duc de Richelieu, to write the British authorities on his behalf. "Mankind and I must thank you for your letter," he congratulated him. "If it doesn't do much good for Admiral Byng, at least it does you much honor." Another unfortunate whose fate preoccupied Voltaire was Thomas-Arthur Lally-Tollendal, the French officer who surrendered Pondichéry to the English. For this he was condemned to death; Voltaire fought for his posthumous rehabilitation, and won.

The very best of *Candide* occurs when the hero and his party land at Portsmouth, coming upon Byng and the firing squad. "Why kill that admiral?" asks Candide. "Because," comes the answer, "he didn't kill enough people; he went into battle against a French admiral and they found he did not get near enough." "But," interrupts Candide, "the French admiral was as far away from the English admiral as the Englishman from the Frenchman." "Quite true," Candide is told, "but in this country it is good from time to time to kill an admiral to encourage the others."

But to overpraise *Candide* is to sell Voltaire short, to forget that he was the unforgettable historian of Louis XIV, the author of the *Mémoires pour Servir à la Vie de M. de Voltaire*, in which so many of the pretentions of the House of Hohenzollern are duly annihilated, and above all the impertinent correspondent of so many famous people who might otherwise be taken seriously.

Like *Zadig* and *Micromégas*, *Candide* is based on the assumption that God is to blame for setting us down in an imperfect world. The assumption makes for monotonous reading, and as satires these three tales cannot compare with *Gulliver's Travels*, where there is even a breath of fantasy, something Voltaire never dared attempt. He could never have conceived of Laputa, the floating island in the sky, the very kind of invention the Surrealist painter Magritte found so congenial in our century. Swift—and who could resist saying this?—was the one writer who might have ruptured the deistical complacency of Madame du Châtelet. How could the "Divine Emilie" reply to Swift's argument against the abolishing of Christianity in England? "If Christianity were once abolished," the argument ran, "How would the Free Thinkers

. . . be able to find another subject so calculated in all points to display their abilities?"

But let us return to *Candide*. André Gide, who took the trouble in 1934 to read it to the very end, down to the decision that "*il faut cultiver notre jardin*," did not rate *Candide* much above the other stories. "I wonder," he asked, "if *Candide* doesn't owe its great fame to the indecent incidents . . . The satire is a trifle thin quite often, and in my opinion the laughter of Voltaire more nearly resembles a grimace. He wrote *Candide* to amuse himself, and in amusing himself he amuses us. But we also feel that he wants to prove something, and we aren't sure exactly what, nor whom he is attacking. You don't need so much wit to prove that man is unconscionably unhappy on earth. Religion teaches us all that, and Voltaire is well aware of this, and sometimes it bothers him."

Rousseau, who claimed he never opened *Candide*, was not delighted by what he heard about the book. "I don't like you at all," he wrote Voltaire in the summer of 1760. "You have done me, your disciple and your enthusiastic admirer, all the harm that could hurt me the most. You have lost me Geneva, that was the price of the asylum you received there, and you have alienated my fellow citizens from me . . . Finally, I hate you. That is what you were after. But I hate you like a man even more worthy of loving you if you so desired. Of all the feelings my heart was filled with for you there remains only the admiration that no one can refuse your beautiful genius, that, and my love for your writings. If I can honor only your tales, the fault is not really mine."

When March came in 1761, Voltaire had not yet recovered. "That arch-madman," he wrote d'Alembert, "who might have amounted to something if he'd been guided by you, has gone off on his own, writes against the theater after producing a bad comedy, writes against France, which supports him, and snatching four or five rotten staves from Diogenes' barrel, throws himself in and begins to bark. After abandoning all his friends, he writes me the most impertinent letter that any fanatic ever scribbled. He tells me in his own words: *You have corrupted Geneva in return for the asylum it provided.* As if I had any desire to improve the morals of Geneva, as if I needed an asylum, as if I sought asylum in that city of socinian preachers, as if I had any obligation whatever to that city!"

Voltaire never delivered his final opinion of Rousseau, but did refer to him, in one scrap of verse, "as the enemy of mankind." The fate of Rousseau was not the only problem on his horizon. The Calas case was coming up, and the Sirven case and the LaBarre case, three opportunities to confound Roman Catholic bigotry and to see that justice was done.

The quarrel between Voltaire and Rousseau may never end. In our own time Gide declared that we only begin to appreciate the importance of Rousseau when we read Voltaire on the subject.

6

A DROP OF SENTIMENT.
NOW AND THEN.

Although Voltaire never said this in so many words, it is obvious that what most displeased him in Christianity was—as he conceived it—its emphasis on sentiment. An awkward, even dangerous preoccupation, sentiment should be banished from civilization. Yet his legal instinct told him it might be useful in winning a case in court. So he turned sentimental when he argued in favor of the Calas and Sirven families and the hapless LaBarre and his confederates. He also had other unsentimental diversions. He tormented a certain LeFranc de Pompignan who made the mistake of taking himself seriously. And he kept on writing plays, destroying in one of them the reputation of Elie Fréron, the critic then doing his best to carry on the campaign of the Abbé Desfontaines. Still another diversion was writing the life of Peter the Great. This, thought Frederick, was a horrid waste of time. Then he cultivated the friendship of Cardinal de Bernis, the churchman who won an immortality all his own in the pages of Casanova.

To begin with the Calas case. Toulouse, in the twentieth century one of the bleak cities of France, was far from cheerful two hundred years ago, a haven for earnest Roman Catholics, fifty thousand strong, who viewed the two hundred Calvinists in their midst with more than misgivings. One of these Calvinists was Jean Calas, a dealer in woolen goods one of whose sons, Louis, had recently gone over to Rome. Another son, Marc-Antoine, hanged himself on the night of October 13, 1761. Since an ordinance dating from 1670 provided that the corpse of any suicide should be dragged through the streets, the Calas family did its best to hush things up. This did no good. Within twenty-four hours after Marc-Antoine's death a warrant was issued for the arrest of his mother, his father, his brother Pierre, one of the family servants, and a friend of the family who happened to be calling that evening. Marc-Antoine was no suicide, said public opinion: he must have been murdered. On March 9, 1762, the parliament of Toulouse, voting eighteen to thirteen, decreed that Jean Calas be broken on the wheel and his son Pierre banished in perpetuity. As for Madame Calas, the neighbor and the family servant, they were released without being declared innocent. Finally, Madame Calas and her daughters were committed to a convent by a *lettre de cachet*.

Voltaire was aware of what was happening before the month of March was over, and one of the first men in whom he confided was the none too devout Roman, François-Joachim de Pierre, Cardinal de Bernis, the very man whom Casanova remembered for sharing the favors of the divine nun M.-M. in Venice. A favorite of Madame de Pompadour, Bernis was a gentleman of consequence. While the French ambassador in Vienna, he laid the groundwork for the Austrian alliance in the Seven Years' War; he was later Secretary of Foreign Affairs until replaced by the Duc de Choiseul in 1758.

"What must I think of the frightful fate of this Calas, put on the wheel at Toulouse for having hanged his son?" Voltaire asked. "People say here that he is very innocent and called God to witness in his dying hour . . . His fate hangs heavy upon me, it saddens me in my pleasures, I feel corrupted. We must look with horror on the parliament of Toulouse, or on the Protestants."

Bernis' first reaction was one of skepticism. "My brother," he wrote back, "who is in Toulouse, hasn't yet got to the bottom of the affair. I don't believe that a Protestant is any more capable of an atrocious crime than a Catholic, but I also can't believe (without looking at the evidence) that our magistrates got together to do a horrible injustice." This was written a week or two before the citizens of Toulouse met to celebrate the two hundredth anniversary of their Protestant massacre. All Huguenots not killed at that time were expelled from the city.

Just before the anniversary fell due, Voltaire sensed that he was being called on stage for one of the great roles of his career. "You may well ask me," he wrote to friends in Paris, "why I am taking such an interest in that Calas they put on the wheel. The reason is that I see so many of our neighbors indignant, and that the Swiss guards in the French service swear they won't fight with any enthusiasm for a nation that, without any proof, puts their brothers on the wheel."

Voltaire was indignant himself. Indignant and cautious. Meticulously he studied the evidence. What was equally important, he lured away from his lovely château in Normandy the exceptional lawyer Elie de Beaumont, who did more than labor for the cause. The greatest names in France should be informed. They were. He also recognized—he was never an idealist—that the Calas family was far from entertaining. In fact they were dull.

One of the dullest was Marc-Antoine's brother Donat, who seems to have taken his good time to defend his father. It was thanks to Voltaire's prodding that he wrote his mother from Switzerland late in June 1762. Voltaire was weeping when he told Donat the news. Donat wept himself on reading his mother's letter to Voltaire. "I fell down on my knees," wrote Donat to his mother. "I prayed God to exterminate me if any member of my family was guilty of the abominable murder ascribed to my father and my brother, and in which you, the best and most virtuous of mothers, have been implicated yourself." Were these Donat's own words? Possibly not. He may have been writing at Voltaire's dictation. We gather our information from Voltaire's pamphlet on the case, issued prior to his *Treatise on Tolerance*, which made the most of the Calas' misfortunes.

There was no doubt about Voltaire's diligence in collecting the facts. Even the Roquefort cheese that the family friend, Gobert Lavaisse, went out to buy on the evening of the crime is duly mentioned. This cheese had its importance, since Lavaisse—to quote the gossip of Toulouse—was the Protestant designated to strangle any member of the sect who dared to desert to Rome. Nor was the hysteria of the populace overlooked. Since the rumor had been spread that Marc-Antoine was about to enter the company of the White Penitents, they were the ones who took charge of the magnificent funeral. The catafalque was splendid. Above it dangled a threatening skeleton, and an ambitious monk was noticed in the act of tearing out the teeth of the corpse. No one listened to the story that Marc-Antoine was all too fond of reading the ancients on the subject of suicide.

Justice, such as it was, was prophesied the instant Marc-Antoine's brother Pierre was led away in chains with his mother and sisters. Pierre had left a lighted torch in the house to make it easier for him to find his way home in the dark. The torch was put out. "You won't be coming home so soon," he was told. And a neighbor swore she had heard Pierre sobbing in the street: "They've killed him with a sword!" "There are," Voltaire pointed out, "great crimes just as there are great virtues: philosophy must repair the damage."

In June Voltaire was composing a petition to Louis XV. "There is no need to go into details," he argued. "We must move the King. This document will cause tears to flow and frighten our readers. If Madame Calas dares to sign this, she is innocent, she and her husband and Pierre and Lavaisse. If not, they are all guilty." She did co-operate and went to Paris in search of justice. She must see Choiseul, the Minister of Foreign Affairs, Voltaire decided, and wrote in her favor to Madame de Pompadour.

Cardinal Bernis was still not convinced. "The sentence is incomprehensible," he admitted, "but there are strange things on both sides." However, Madame de Pompadour saw the light. "The case of this unfortunate man Calas makes me shudder," she wrote in August 1762. "We are sorry he was born a Huguenot, but all the same we shouldn't treat him like a highwayman. It seems impossible that he was guilty of the crime of which he was accused; that would be unnatural. But he is dead, his family is under a curse, and his judges show no sign of repenting. The kind heart of the King has suffered over this strange adventure, and all of France cries for vengeance. The poor man will be revenged, although we cannot bring him back to life. These people in Toulouse have lost all control of themselves, and are much more religious in their own style than they need to become good Christians. May God convert them and make them more human!"

About this time Voltaire discovered that Madame Calas was an imbecile of a Huguenot. "But that does not make her any less innocent, nor the sentence of Toulouse any less abominable," he pleaded. He had already succeeded in upsetting the Duc de Choiseul, who did not enjoy his latest letter to d'Alembert on this subject. "It is all very well," said Choiseul, "to complain about injustice, but do be prudent. You must not keep on complaining as you are doing, and there is no point in making enemies for yourself in order to play the game of lawyer for lost causes."

Of course Voltaire persevered, and on March 9, 1765, the Royal Council rehabilitated the Calas family. The joy in Paris was universal, Voltaire reported, who noted that the family, whose property had been confiscated, was now presented with £36,000, 3,000 of which was allocated to their loyal Catholic servant. Louis, he proclaimed, deserved to be called the "well-beloved" for this deed. He ended his *Treatise on Tolerance* with the hope that all men would remember that they are brothers: "If you want to imitate Jesus Christ, be martyrs, not executioners."

The Calas case was one opportunity. Another was the Sirven case. On January 4, 1762, Elisabeth Sirven, the daughter of a Protestant authority on feudal law in the town of Castres (about halfway between Toulouse and Carcasonne) was found dead at the bottom of a well. She was known to be mentally deranged, she had once been kidnapped by Romans counting on her conversion, and she had been sent home by the Romans as an apparently hopeless case. These were the facts. Which did not prevent the local bigots from crying out that she had been murdered. Two weeks after her body was discovered, the warrant for the arrest of the entire family was issued. They had the intelligence to flee town at once, but the law would have its way and on March 29, 1764 the family was sentenced. Pierre-Paul Sirven and his wife were to be hanged and their two daughters obliged to witness the execution and then banished. In the absence of the accused, they were all hanged in effigy. Sirven appealed to the Royal Council early in 1767 but to no avail. At last, on August 31, 1769, he surrendered to the authorities and was put in prison pending a new appeal. Two months later his guilt was reaffirmed by the courts, although the sentence was reduced to a fine and banishment. Finally, on November 25, 1771, a new parliament was installed and the Sirvens acquitted of all the accusations brought against them. This acquittal was four times reaffirmed.

Even though Voltaire was aware of this new miscarriage of justice as early as December 1763, he quite naturally took his time before entering the argument: the Calas family came first. But by February 1765 he was writing Beaumont that the Sirvens had escaped to Switzerland and misery. We might as well be living in the time of the Albigensian heresy, he decided. In the next month he was telling a friend in Paris that Elisabeth Sirven had been whipped in the convent to encourage her to memorize the catechism. She then threw herself into the well, and the zealots had no doubt that her father, mother, and sisters drowned her. And now the Sirvens were at his door. "Just imagine, my dear friend, four sheep accused by the butchers of devouring a lamb! . . . How can I describe so much innocence and so much horror . . . I have been following as usual my own inclination: that of a *philosophe* is not to take pity on the unfortunate, but to be of use to them."

"Defender of innocence, conqueror of fanaticism, O man born to make people happy!" he wrote Beaumont in the spring of 1765. "I believe you now have all the necessary information to come to the rescue of the wretched Sirven family." All their property had vanished, he emphasized.

Madame Sirven has just died of her grief, he notified a friend in Paris that June. This was most unfortunate, for he was counting on her testimony to determine certain important facts. "I realize," he told another friend, "that this little play can't be as sensational as the Calas tragedy, but we aren't looking for a hit, we only want justice." He did collect two hundred ducats from ex-King Stanislas of Poland and five hundred pounds from Frederick and even hinted to Cardinal Bernis that he too should join the crusade.

"The great work of the Church seems to me rather boring," he confessed to Bernis, "but you are doing good, you are loved, and you should rejoice in your good deeds, as the book of Ecclesiastes tells us, that book wrongly attributed to Solomon." But the cardinal prized Voltaire the writer more than Voltaire the evangelist, "If you send me some verses, take care that I may be proud of them," he answered. "I am neither a pedant nor a hypocrite, but surely you would be annoyed if I weren't all that I must be and seem . . . Prolong your sunset, decorate it by laughing at ridiculous things, and by teaching young writers and setting them an example, while giving pleasure to your friends. Goodbye, my dear colleague, I love you as much as I admire you."

Possibly Voltaire was overworked on the day he simplified the history of Christianity for the benefit of a Swiss Huguenot. "There is," he wrote, "an abominable monster abroad who brought about the unhappiness of the Calases and Sirvens after having spread its poisons in the world for more than sixteen hundred years. This is the monster we must crush. It is true that this dragon was born of a respectable mother, but it is tearing its mother to pieces, and we must strike it on its breast." The day was fortunately drawing near when Voltaire's secretary could advise the Sirven girls that their father was released from prison.

The next victim in whom Voltaire took an interest was hardly so interesting. Jean-François-Lefèvre LaBarre, from all the evidence at our disposal, seems to have been a flippant creature, perhaps as great a bigot as the bigoted Roman Catholics who cheered his execution. Voltaire presumed he might have enjoyed a splendid career in the army. This is most unlikely, although his grandfather had been a lieutenant general. In the village of Abbeville in Picardy he was notorious, not for his study of tactics but for his scoffing at the rites of the Church. As for his reading, it was mainly confined to novels like *La Religieuse en Chemise, Le Portier des Chartreux,* and other spice for the immature. He did own a copy of Voltaire's *Dictionnaire Philosophique* and was fond of reciting bawdy bits from *La Pucelle.* His reverence for licentious and anticlerical literature was certainly sincere. Rumor had it that he piled his favorite books on an improvised altar and knelt before them.

His troubles began on the night of August 8, 1765, when the Romans of Abbeville discovered that a crucifix on the Pont-Neuf had been mutilated and another crucifix in the cemetery of Sainte-Catherine profaned and covered with filth. Voltaire, as you may have guessed, felt that the only proper place for a crucifix was inside a church, never in the open.

From the first, suspicion centered on a certain Gaillard d'Etallonde, who with LaBarre had made a point of refusing to doff his hat before a religious procession. What was the host, claimed LaBarre, but a bit of wax? Living with his aunt, the Abbess of Willancourt, LaBarre succeeded in separating her from the affecttions of a rich miser by the name of Belleval. The jilted Belleval now ran from house to house denouncing LaBarre for his impious behavior. He also rounded up whatever witnesses he could to testify. And when he found out that his own son had joined LaBarre's circle, spirited him out of town. Although Belleval was cordially disliked, he saw to it that LaBarre, who strangely enough had sought refuge in a neighboring abbey, was brought to trial. In the meantime d'Etallonde, denounced as the real culprit by LaBarre and another member of the group, escaped to freedom.

Was LaBarre actually guilty of the desecration? Even if he were, thought Voltaire, a year in prison would have been punishment enough. The court decided otherwise, and the verdict came close to justifying Voltaire's misgivings concerning Christianity. La-Barre was sentenced to have his tongue cut out, his head cut off, and his body burned. To the end he was intransigeant. He refused to offer any apology at the door of Saint-Wulfram's Church and after having his legs broken under torture argued his tormentors out of slicing out his tongue. When they shaved off his hair, he grew impatient. "Do you want to make a choir boy out of me?" he asked. To a priest standing beside him he murmured: "I didn't believe that they could send a gentleman to his death for such a little thing." When it was all over, they tossed the *Dictionnaire Philosophique* into the flames.

Voltaire must have understood that LaBarre made an awkward candidate for immortality, but did the best he could for d'Etallonde, recommending him to Frederick's armed forces. For a few days, thinking of LaBarre's fate and that of the *Dictionnaire,* Voltaire trembled. He even thought of abandoning Ferney for a colony of Free Thinkers that Frederick might establish. To his new friend Catherine the Great he wrote: "The abominable punishment of LaBarre, of which Your Imperial Majesty has heard, and at which she must have shuddered, so unnerved me that I was on the point of leaving France and returning to the King of Prussia. But today I think I should rather end my days in a greater empire than his."

Voltaire was not to settle in either Berlin or Saint Petersburg, but did maintain a quite objective point of vew during the Seven Years' War. Frederick might be the enemy of France, but not exactly the enemy of Voltaire. Routed by the Austrians at Kolín on June 18, 1757, Frederick for a time seriously considered the joy of suicide, comparing himself to Cato of Utica, who took his life in 46 B.C. rather than face the victorious Julius Ceasar. This dramatic pose did not please the dramatist of Ferney. "If," Voltaire wrote him, "your luck did not hold, if your courage in unfortunate circumstances that I cannot foresee, rose to the heroic heights that were honored in ancient times, still your resolution would not be approved today." Frederick's spirits improved on November 5, when the Prussians smashed the French led by the Maréchal de Soubise at Rossbach.

During the Seven Years' War entertainment was as necessary as ever. In the fall of 1761 Voltaire dashed off in six days the tragedy of *Olympie*, congratulating himself on the speed at which he worked. "It took only six days," he reminded d'Alembert, who reminded him that the author should have rested on the seventh. Cardinal Bernis agreed. "I am sending you back your six-day work," he wrote. "I believe that when you will have spent six days improving the style of this play, using instead of the very first phrases that come to you in the heat of composition, more appropriate and less stale lines, this work will be worthy of you and of the affection you bear it."

Bernis was a critic who counted, for he grew close to Pope Clement XIV. "What a good head your Pope has!" Voltaire wrote him shortly after His Holiness's elevation. "Since he has been in office, he hasn't done anything silly." This was reported to Clement XIV, who appeared to be flattered. "If you end up as a good Capuchin monk, the Pope will dare to love you as much as he esteems you," Bernis declared. Such was his sophistication that the cardinal looked forward to the day Voltaire would return to the faith. "Like most of my colleagues," he confessed on another occasion, "I can't believe that you aim to banish religion from the face of the earth. You have always been the enemy of fanaticism, and you must be aware that, if fanaticism fighting in defense of religion is dangerous, equally dangerous is the fanaticism that seeks to destroy religion."

A more significant drama than *Olympie* was *Tancrède*, even if, like all of Voltaire's plays, it has been overlooked by the twentieth century. Today it is remembered if at all only because it inspired the libretto for the opera by Rossini in 1813. Much, however, was made of *Tancrède* when it was first staged, and Mademoiselle Clairon gave a dazzling performance as Aménaïde in this evocation of mediaeval Syracuse. The dedication, to Madame de Pompadour, was one of those mistakes. Voltaire could not refrain from mentioning her old protégé, the dramatist Crébillon, for whom, as everyone knew, he had no use whatever.

But on the death of Madame de Pompadour in the spring of 1764, Voltaire remembered her for what she might have been. "Do you miss her?" he asked d'Alembert. "Yes, no doubt, for at the bottom of her heart, she was on our side; she stood up, as much as she could, for the literary profession . . . It is all a beautiful dream, long since past."

Voltaire may have been bored now and then by the longer articles of the *Encyclopédie*, but could not resist, in the spring of 1760, only a month or two before the première of *Tancrède*, the temptation of demolishing the Marquis de Pompignan, who used the occasion of his acceptance speech at the Academy to ridicule the labors of d'Alembert and his co-workers. Trained, like Voltaire, at Louis-le-Grand, Pompignan made a conscientious magistrate and a conscientious poet. He was the author of an ode to old Jean-Baptiste Rousseau and also of the drama *Didon*. But he was not noted for his humor, and when disciplined for his high-mindedness as judge, compared his exile to that of Ovid. The academician he was replacing was Maupertuis, who had returned to the Roman Catholic faith in his old age. Perhaps it was this fact that led him to launch an attack in his speech on "those base and troubling characters eager to undermine the throne and the altar." Voltaire himself was not named but was revealed as the creator of "impious systems, insolent verses, and scandalous libels."

At once Voltaire went into action. "When one has the honor," he wrote, "of being received into a respectable society of men of letters, the address one delivers must not be a satire against men of letters: that would be an insult to the society and to the public

. . . When one is admitted into a respectable group, one must conceal under the veil of modesty that insolent pride that one associates with idiots and people devoid of all talent."

This was not all. Pompignan's translation of the psalms had made everyone yawn; no one should forget this. Besides, it was a point of particular importance to Voltaire. He had once been urged to turn the psalms into French for the edification of Madame de Pompadour in a pious interval, an opportunity he declined.

Pompignan was easily erased. He was not even a warm enemy. This title was claimed by Elie-Catherin Fréron, another graduate of Louis-le-Grand, who considered himself, with some justice, to be the perfect replacement for the Abbé Desfontaines. He was even employed for a time by Desfontaines. "I have," said the unrelenting Fréron, "nothing much to say about the talent of the famous Voltaire. And I should have even less to say about him if he had kept to writing verses, the only thing he is capable of."

Although Madame du Deffand considered Fréron to be an improvement on Desfontaines and said so to Voltaire, he may not have agreed. He liked to remember that Fréron cheated at cards and had spent some time in prison for libeling Cardinal Bernis. And what Voltaire read in Fréron's publication L'Année Littéraire did not dispose him to benevolence. The public was told, for example, that Voltaire could not possibly be the author of Candide: a clever monkey had simply been using his name. Voltaire, he went on, was really only a French author, that is he belonged to his century and his country, while real poets belong to the ages and to every country. All this led Voltaire to pay particular attention to Fréron's relations with a niece of his. She "became his housekeeper and he got two children by her; during her second pregnancy he married her to keep her quiet."

Fréron's execution could not be postponed. Voltaire went to the exquisite trouble of sticking him under the name Frélon (or hornet) in a comedy Le Café ou l'Ecossaise that he staged at the Comédie Française in the summer of 1760. The thing was a hoax worthy of his talent. The presumed author was a certain Hume, a pastor in Edinburgh and a cousin of the philosopher. The presumed translator was a certain Jérôme Carré of Montauban.

The plot concerned the adventures of Lindane, a Scottish girl finally allowed to marry a Scotsman, the son of a deadly enemy of her family. But Fréron or Frélon plays the leading role. He is a nasty journalist, given to saying things like, "We must hiss any play that goes over, and never tolerate anything first rate." The première was glorious. Fréron himself was in the audience, as was his wife, and they were obliged to listen to cries of "Down with Fréron!" from the *philosophes* who packed the theater.

The only worry of Voltaire at this time was the production that very spring of Charles Palissot de Montenoy's comedy *Les Philosophes*, which Diderot regarded as a deadly insult. For Palissot intimated that Diderot and his associates might be guilty of hoodwinking naive Parisians. Thinly disguised as Dortidius, Diderot is not above praising his own books in society. As for the French public, it does not amount to much in his eyes:

> *Je m'embarrasse peu du pays que j'habite,*
> *Le véritable sage est cosmopolite . . .*

[*I worry little about the country I am living in,/The really wise man is a cosmopolitan . . .*]

Nor is Rousseau forgotten. The valet Crispin, pretending to be Jean-Jacques, comes on stage on all fours:

> *En nous civilisant, nous avons tout perdu . . .*

[*In becoming civilized, we have lost everything . . .*]

Voltaire was omitted from the cast. This he should have relished, but the very fact that he was not ridiculed caused him some concern. "You should have been the friend of the *philosophes* instead of writing against them," he told Palissot. "I must confess that I wish you could have spared Monsieur Diderot. He has been persecuted, and he is an unhappy man. This should endear him to all men of letters." Palissot could not agree. "The mediocre and detestable side of Monsieur Diderot far outweighs anything first rate in his works," he answered.

By this time Voltaire was deep in the biography of Peter the Great, commissioned by the Russian government in 1757. This book could not be compared to *Charles XII*. Having already surveyed the rivalry of the two rulers, all he could do in this new work was to concentrate on the founding of Saint Petersburg and attempt to penetrate the picturesque darkness of Russian history. But when the book was finished, Voltaire found his reward: the friendship of Catherine the Great, who came to the throne in 1762, following the convenient murder of her husband, Peter III.

Voltaire wasted little sympathy on Peter III. The Russia of Catherine the Great was close to paradise. "I never wanted to go to Rome," he told Catherine in 1766. "I always had a certain reluctance to observe all those monks in the Capitol and to think of the tombs of the Scipios trampled upon by priests. But I am sick with regret that I can't see the deserts of your land transformed into superb cities." She became one of his favorite correspondents in his old age.

She was not one to resent the never-ending rain of compliments from Ferney. "He was my master," she told her German friend Friedrich Melchior Grimm a few months after Voltaire's death. "It was he, or rather, his works, that formed my intellect and my judgment. I am his pupil; when I was younger, I loved to please him; before I was satisfied with any action it had to be worthy of being reported to him, and I informed him of it immediately."

7

A MURDER SHOULD NEVER
COME BETWEEN FRIENDS

A murder should never come between friends. Only rarely would Voltaire admit that Catherine was guilty of impatience on her way to the throne. "I believe," he once confessed to d'Alembert, "that the time may have come for us to moderate our enthusiasm for the North. It does produce some strange philosophers." But this mood passed. He was determined to spend a serene old age. There was no point in quarreling with an empress. He could pick quarrels of his own with lesser figures. Besides, at all times he must be ready to receive his distinguished guests at Ferney. And nothing must be allowed to interfere with all the letters exchanged with Madame du Deffand.

She could tell him, in the fall of 1759, that "I don't like to feel that the author I'm reading is set to write a book. I like to imagine that he's holding a conversation with me." The author must not let the conversation drag; in that case she would be bored. Boredom, not the loss of her eyesight, was the curse of her existence. Who could be more boring than the perpetrators of the *Encylopédie*? "I shall always be charmed to have your advice," she admitted. "Give me a prescription against boredom; that's what I need. Searching for the truth is the perfect panacea for you and for me, too, but not quite in the same sense. You believe you have discovered the truth. I think it can't be discovered. As for your modern philosophers, there never was anyone less philosophical and less tolerant. They'd like to crush everyone who won't kneel down before them. I know them all too well."

Voltaire would then remind her that he was no atheist on the order of Diderot. "You must be convinced how far away I am from certain modern philosophers who deny a supreme intelligence, creator of all worlds. I can't conceive of how such clever mathematicians deny an eternal mathematician. That wasn't the way of Newton and Plato. The only thing I have in common with the modern philosophers is their horror of intolerant fanaticism."

Then she would return to the argument. "Your philosophers," she would tease him, "or rather, your so-called philosophers, are cold characters, pompous fellows without a cent to their name, timid souls who have never enjoyed a brave moment, preaching equality because they hope to dominate the scene . . ."

He yearned to confuse her but could never quite succeed. "I must scold you," he would write her. "Why do you hate the philosophers when you think just the way they do? You should be their queen and you make yourself their enemy. I know you are dissatisfied with one of them"—a reference to d'Alembert—"but why must all of them suffer? Must you outlaw your own subjects? One of my articles of faith, Madame, is to believe that you have a superior mind. My charity consists in loving you even if you no longer love me."

"I don't hate philosophy at all," she would counter, "but I have no use for those who use it as a mask under which they conceal their pride and their insolence. You are no more fond than I of paradoxes, boring reasoning, and a cold, bland, declamatory style. It is your own fault if I have become difficult. Do you imagine that I'm going to read all the stuff with which we are assailed? To force me to read all this trash, they tell me that some of it is yours. I dip into all this, I can't recognize you anywhere, and I throw everything into the fire."

Helvétius, she found, was to be avoided at any cost. "They tell me you've found some pearls and diamonds in this little brochure of his. As I can't live long enough to read this, and my life might even be shortened by dying of boredom, please show me the pages that include these precious stones . . . So," she added, "*these* are the precious diamonds of Helvétius! And there are a thousand more, you tell me. My dear Voltaire, can't you recognize these beautiful diamonds for what they are, the stones from your garden? . . . I admire your patience in reading the most boring books in the world."

Then she would capture Voltaire once again. "Have pity on me," she wrote him in the summer of 1769. "All living writers bore me, give me the names of a few poets who may amuse me. I have read twenty times over the books I like, and I always have to go back to them. I'd like to get one of your pamphlets once a week, I'm persuaded you could take care of the expense. I believe there is just so much imagination in every century, distributed in the different nations. By some subtle means you have got hold of this, and haven't left a touch for anyone else. Now it is up to you to distribute your holdings, and in your generosity you must think of your good old friend."

She was not above telling him that he was the very center of the universe—the idol of the universe. "You have an enchanting style," she went on. "I was saying the other day that I shouldn't be annoyed if they condemned me to read only one author, provided that I had my choice, and added that I must have been so condemned, because I could no longer read anyone but you . . . I find that your old age is a kind of apotheosis. You have become a god in your own lifetime. Ferney is a temple to which they come from all over the universe to pay you homage."

There were times when Voltaire guessed what she was about. "In spite of all her good sense, she is still a woman," he decided. "She flirts with me, she teases me, she turns my head, and when she is sure she has inspired a serious passion, she drops me."

She was so close to Voltaire that she could not resist giving him all the news of her dearest friend, the Duchesse de Choiseul. The grand-daughter of the immensely rich banker Crozat le Pauvre, who made his millions out of Louisiana, Louise-Honorine de Choiseul was the patient spectator of the wayward glances of her spendthrift husband, who made his impression on Madame de Pompadour and so became ambassador to the Vatican and then to Vienna and ultimately was made Minister of Foreign Affairs during the Seven Years' War. Dismissed in 1770 at the whim of Madame du Barry, he was sent into exile at Chanteloup, his estate in the Loire Valley. Madame de Deffand was to visit the Choiseuls in exile again and again. "It is a shame she is an angel," she said of Louise-Honorine. "I'd rather she were a woman, but she has only virtues, not a single weakness, not a single fault."

Madame de Choiseul had her own opinion of Voltaire. "He has always been a coward even when he wasn't in danger, insolent with no good reason, and a low creature with no ideals. But," she told Madame du Deffand, "that doesn't stop him from being the most brilliant man of the century. We must admire his talents, stuff our heads with his writings, enlighten our minds with his philosophy, and learn from him about morality. We must burn incense before him and we must despise him. That is the fate of nearly all our objects of worship." She added: "What other author can tell me as he can what everyone knows?"

These were the days when Voltaire was writing Madame du Deffand: "Be often bored, Madame, for then you will write me. The beautiful soul of the Duc de Choiseul protects us. I don't know any more generous and noble heart than his, for in spite of what Jean-Jacques says, we have some good men in the government."*

Voltaire was to disappoint the company at Chanteloup on Christmas Eve, 1774. The subtle harpsichordist Balbastre was to play a Christmas suite on the Choiseul piano, and Madame du Deffand longed for a Christmas poem from Ferney. The verses that arrived were most unsatisfactory. "Why do you treat me like this?" she asked. "If you had turned me down, it would have been better than this sort of kindness. This is all the thanks you'll receive." Voltaire did make another try. "You should have said," he pointed out, "that no crèches were called for, or Jesus or Mary, although they are really essential. You should know that when it comes to carols, there is no salvation outside of the Church. Nobody could guess what you wanted. Women are tyrants, but they should at least spell out their wishes."

---

*This was a Monday morning judgment. By Tuesday Voltaire might find much to criticize in Choiseul.

Death proved to be a more congenial topic. "Let's have some common sense on the subject," he argued. "It is certain that we don't know what it feels like, it is not necessarily painful, it ressembles sleep like two peas, the only trouble is the idea that one won't wake up. The horrible thing is the ceremony of death, the barbarity of extreme unction, and the cruelty of warning us that all is over." Madame du Deffand had to agree. "The less one thinks and reflects, the happier one is . . . You will never know what unhappiness is all about, and as I have already told you, when one has a good mind and a certain talent, one can find great resources in oneself. *Il faut être Voltaire ou végéter* (One must be Voltaire or vegetate)." His mind was made up. "When I think everything over," he told her, "I believe that we must never think of death at all. The very idea is enough to poison our lives . . . The people who make so much of death are the enemies of mankind. We must never let them come near us. Death is nothing at all. Only the idea of death is sad. Let's never think about it and live from day to day."

But they could never be of one mind on the subject of Catherine. In the spring of 1767 he told Madame du Deffand that the "Semiramis of the North"—he often likened her to the ancient Assyrian princess—was sending fifty thousand troops into Poland to establish liberty of conscience. "This," he proclaimed, "is unique in the history of the world. I must brag to you a little that I am in her good graces: I stand as her knight against the world. I know that people hold against her a few trifles concerning her husband, but those are family matters that are not my business. Besides, it is not a bad thing to make a mistake for which one must offer an apology. That means that one must make every effort to win the esteem and admiration of the people, and certainly that fool husband of hers would never have accomplished any of the great things Catherine does every day."

"You are so fond of your Catherine that you might try to call on her, and that would be insane," Madame du Deffand replied. "Never look at her except through the telescope of your imagination, write a beautiful novel about her, make her as interesting as the Semiramis of that tragedy of yours, but always leave between you two a geographical distance."

Holding his ground, Voltaire reminded Madame du Deffand that "they speak a purer French at the court of the Empress than at Versailles, because our beautiful ladies have never bothered to study grammar." But she remained unconvinced. "I can't admire your Catherine," she told him. "She is nothing but ostentation, she buys pictures, diamonds, and libraries to astonish the universe with her wealth. She doesn't levy any taxes, but you know as well as I that where there is no cash on hand, the ruler loses his rights. She has increased the pay of her troops, but pays them only in paper. You are much too pleased with her admiration for you. Who doesn't admire you? I beg your pardon for my impertinence, but you know where I acquired it."

Horace Walpole, kept in touch by Madame du Deffand, admitted that he too was shocked. "Voltaire makes me sick with his Catherine," he decided in the summer of 1767. "The assassination of a husband and the usurpation of a throne make a beautiful subject for a jest. He says it is not a bad idea to make a mistake for which one must offer an apology. How does one apologize for a murder? Do you do it by hiring poets? By hiring mercenary historians and by bribing ridiculous philosophers a thousand leagues away from her country? Those are the vile souls who sing hymns to an Augustus and keep quite about the men he exiles. Ambition causes crimes," he concluded. "Avarice canonizes crimes."

Walpole could hardly forgive Catherine for acquiring so many old masters from the collection at Houghton, his father's seat in Norfolk. What were her acquisitions but the advertisement of unhappy days for the Walpole family? Nor could he excuse Voltaire's liberty in ridiculing the gravediggers' scene in *Hamlet*. "Unhappy Shakespeare!" Walpole murmured in the second preface to his Gothic romance, *The Castle of Otranto*, a copy of which was forwarded to Ferney. He noticed that Voltaire made much of a couplet of Racine "which, to my English ears, always sounded as the flattest and most trifling instance of circumstantial propriety."

De son appartement cette porte est prochaine,
Et cette autre conduit dans celui de la reine.

In Walpole's English this became:

> *To Caesar's closet through this door you come,*
> *And t'other leads to the Queen's drawing-room.*

Walpole realized he should apologize for daring to contradict Voltaire. "Without knowing it," he explained, "you have been my master, and perhaps the sole merit that may be found in my writings is owing to my having studied yours . . . I was not a stranger to your reputation very many years ago, but remember to have then thought you honored our house by dining with my mother—though I was at school, and had not the happiness of seeing you: and yet my father was in a situation that might have dazzled eyes older than mine. The plain name of that father, and the pride of having had so excellent a father, to whose virtues truth at last does justice, is all I have to boast."

Here was a letter that Voltaire could not ignore. "You have made your nation believe that I despise Shakespeare," he answered on July 15, 1768. "I am the man who discovered Shakespeare for the French . . . A long time ago I said that if Shakespeare had appeared in the century of Addison, he would have added to his genius the elegance and the purity that make Addison worthy of respect. I said that his genius belongs to him, his faults to his century."

"The admirable letter you have been so good as to send me is a proof that you are one of those truly great and rare men who know at once how to conquer and how to pardon," Walpole replied, in what reads like a parody of Voltaire's flattering royalty. "One can never be sorry to have been in the wrong, when one's errors are pointed out to one in so obliging and masterly a manner. Whatever opinion I may have of Shakespeare, I should think him to blame, if he could have seen the letter you have done me the honor to write to me, and yet not conform to the rules you have there laid down. When he lived, there had not been a Voltaire both to give laws to the stage, and to show on what good sense those laws were founded. Your art, Sir, goes still farther: for you have supported your arguments without having recourse to the best authority, your own works."

Walpole did not take the trouble to remind Voltaire that he was not joining his efforts to undermine Christianity. "Freethinking is for oneself, surely not for society" may sum up his reaction to the new French philosophers. He sensed that Madame du Deffand would be the first to agree with him. "She corresponds with Voltaire," he informed the poet Thomas Gray, "dictates charming letters to him, contradicts him, is no bigot to him or anybody, and laughs both at the clergy and the philosophers. In a dispute, into which she easily falls, she is very warm, yet scarce ever in the wrong: her judgment on every subject is as just as possible; on every point of conduct as wrong as possible." She relished, and this could not have surprised Walpole, the letter he faked from Frederick the Great to Rousseau: "Show your enemies that sometimes you may have common sense; that will make them angry and do you no harm." So ran this invitation to come live in Prussia. Walpole was later to wonder whether he had not been mean in this instance.

Although Voltaire did not begin to devote the attention to Dante that he did to Shakespeare, he was puzzled by the Italian's reputation. "You want to know about Dante?" he asked himself in a memorandum. "The Italians call him divine, but his divinity is concealed from us. Very few people comprehend this oracle. He has his commentators—one more excuse for not being understood. His reputation will keep on growing because almost no one reads him. There are twenty or so quotations which everyone knows by heart. So there really is no reason to examine the rest of his work."

Was it the ecstasy of being in touch with Catherine that led him to neglect the study of Dante? By the summer of 1766 he was beginning to release the torrent of his devotion. "All eyes must now turn toward the North Star," he informed her. "Your Imperial Majesty has discovered a road to glory until this time unrevealed to other sovereigns. Before now no one had thought of spreading benevolence over seven or eight hundred leagues. You have indeed become the benefactress of Europe, and you have acquired more subjects by the grandeur of your soul than others by feats of arms." So he saluted her victories over the Turks and the coming first partition of Poland. Her generosity had already overwhelmed the Calas family. Would she be so kind as to remember the Sirvens as well?

"Monsieur," she answered, "the light of the North Star is only the Aurora Borealis. These benefactions over so many hundred leagues . . . they are not mine. The Calases owe everything to their friends . . . How could I refuse to send a modest gift to the Sirvens? Do you intend to praise me for this? Is there any need to?"

"May Your Imperial Majesty forgive me," he begged. "You are not at all the Aurora Borealis, you are most certainly the most brilliant star in the North, and no one has ever been so beneficent as you. Andromeda, Perseus, and Calisto can't come anywhere near you. All those stars would have let Diderot die of starvation." This was his way of alluding to the fact that she had bought Diderot's library, giving him the life use. "He has been persecuted in his own country, and your charity has sought him out. Louis XIV had less magnificence than Your Majesty." Nor was this all that he had to say. A month or two later he opened another stop. "The time will come, Madame, I keep on saying this, when all light will come to us from the North. In spite of what Your Imperial Majesty has to say on the subject, I insist you are a star, and you will remain a star."

His attentions did not pass unnoticed in Saint Petersburg. "I begged you about a year ago," she wrote him at the end of 1768, "to send me everything that was ever written by the author whose works I like best of all to read. Last May I got the package I wanted, accompanied by the bust of the most illustrious man of our century, around whose neck I hung an order of knighthood of as brilliant a hue as the imagination of the man the marble represented . . . But until now I haven't acknowledged this gift or thanked you. This is what I thought. A scrap of paper with something scribbled in bad French is a sterile way to thank such a man. I'd like to send you some verses in return for yours, but a woman who isn't bright enough to write good verses is better off working with her hands. Here's what I've done: I've made a tobacco pouch which I beg you to accept. It bears the stamp of the person who has the highest esteem for you."

All this while he never forgot that Frederick as well enjoyed praise. "For some time I've been telling you that you are the most extraordinary man who ever lived," he told him in the winter of 1759. 'Taking on all of Europe and then writing the verses Your Majesty sends me, that is really unique." Not long after this he was writing an old friend in Paris: "What is this you are telling me about *Luke*? Don't you know that he is capable of anything? He is a madman who goes from one extreme to the other. Good and evil are ever-present." *Luke* was the name of the pet monkey at Ferney, a vicious animal who dearly loved to sink his teeth into unwary guests. Voltaire could not have been displeased to hear from Madame du Deffand that Frederick's poetry was as insufferable as ever. The Duc de Choiseul was also unimpressed by Frederick the poet. "I have never read anything so boring in my life," he claimed.

With the years Frederick was no more charming than ever. "People are still talking about the niece of Molière," he advised Voltaire—and incidentally, Madame Denis—"but no one will ever talk about the niece of Voltaire, because she is nothing but an hors d'oeuvre." He added: "Your nation is the most unreliable in Europe. It is clever enough, but rambles on and on when it comes to ideas."

The two were destined to be reasonable rather than firm friends. "The verb *haîr* (hate) will never have two syllables in the indicative case," Voltaire explained in the winter of 1767. For his part Frederick made plain that "You've done me all the mischief you could. I've suffered all that I could, and if I say nothing about the just complaints I have to offer about your conduct, it is because I am capable of forgiveness." To this sort of thing Voltaire might answer: "I shall never console myself for the misfortune which makes me end my days far from you."

He could imagine Frederick's pleasure in 1775 in welcoming the great actor LeKain, who performed in one play after another by the master, and could also smile at Potsdam's verdict that LeKain was too bombastic: he had been trained at Ferney.

"Our Germans," Frederick confided in an amiable moment, "are ambitious to become judges of the fine arts. They are trying to equal Athens, Rome, Florence, and Paris. In spite of my love of my country, I can't say they have succeeded up to now. They are lacking in two things: a language and taste. The language is too prolix; people who have any manners speak French, and a few pedants and a few professors can't teach us politeness and good manners—things that may only be acquired in the great world. Then think of all the dialects! Each province must have its own, and up to now there is no agreement about which to prefer. As for taste, the Germans have none at all."

Frederick's own taste was revealed in his discussion of the sacrament of Holy Communion. "You must admit," he wrote in the spring of 1776, "that neither in antiquity nor in any nation in the world had anyone imagined a more atrocious and blasphemous absurdity than that of eating God. This is the most revolting dogma of the Christian religion, the most hurtful to the Supreme Being, the height of madness and dementia."

Reverence for Christ was not required in Potsdam. When Frederick learned, in the spring of 1777, that Maria Theresa's son Joseph II was nearing Geneva, he thought it was understood that he would call on Voltaire. "I expect," said Frederick, "he'll pass through Ferney and that he'll want to meet and hear the man of the century, the Virgil and Cicero of our time. If that happens, you will put Jesus in his place."

But it did not happen. The Count of Falkenstein (Joseph II was traveling incognito) dashed by Ferney without stopping, even though exquisite preparations were made for his coming. Voltaire put on his finest wig, ordered the finest dinner possible, and took the precaution of having all the stones removed from the highway that ran to Versoix. The humiliation was impossible to conceal, for the count made a point of calling on the painter Liotard in Geneva and also inspected the natural history cabinet of Professor de Saussure.

Americans were more respectful. The fullest account of an American visit to Ferney comes from John Morgan, the Philadelphia physician responsible for introducing the cult of the umbrella to the New World. He and his fellow Philadelphian Samuel Powel could scarcely complain of their reception in September 1764.

"He asked," wrote Morgan to Samuel Morris back home, "why we had not come out time eno' to dine with him, and why we made any difficulties, for, says he, you know, gentlemen, that sitting together at table opens ye heart and makes one more sprightly and sociable. Although at a loss sometimes for an English word, and that he used many Gallicisms, yet he took pains to articulate his words properly and accent them fully . . . We met with few Frenchmen who pronounce English better . . .

"His introduction of us was to this effect: I beg leave to present to you two English gentlemen—oh, glorious nation, renowned conquerors of Canada! Though they have fought against you, and well have they fought battles by land and sea, we must now look upon them as our brave friends, since we are now at peace . . .

"A little dog happening to cross the room stopped before Mr. Voltaire, wagged his tail and seemed to notice him very attentively. On which Mr. Voltaire turned to Mr. Powel, and as I thought a little abruptly, asked him: What do you think of that little dog? Has he a soul or not, and what do people in England now think of the soul?" This seems to have put Powel off. "To show that he was not desirous of enlarging upon this topic, his answer was that the people of England now as well as heretofore entertained very different notions from each other concerning the soul . . ."

Voltaire went on. "The English, added he, have some very fine authors, they are, I swear by God himself, the first nation in Europe, and if I ever smell of a resurrection, or come a second time on earth, I will pray God to make me born in England, the land of liberty. These are four things which I adore that the English boast of so greatly—with his forefinger of the right hand counting them up, and naming each distinctly and with an emphasis: *Liberty, Property, Newton and Locke* . . .

"He begins now to stoop with years or care, is thin, meager and if straight I believe would be about five feet ten inches high. Has a very sagacious but at the same time comical look. Something satirical and very lively in his action, of which he is as full as most of his nation are . . .

"He conducted us into the garden, and pointing to the Lake of Geneva within about half a league or perhaps a little more— there, says he, is the Thames—and there is Richmond Hill, showing us the hills of Savoy beyond the lake—and those vineyards all

around this garden and the verdant lawns are Greenwich. You
see, I am quite in the English taste. Look at the woods. There you
see a road in the woods, another in the vineyard. In the garden
you have plain gravel walks or green lawns—no French gew-
gaws. All is after nature."

Voltaire, who seems to have been suffering from an hallucina-
tion when he claimed that he was living in the English taste, was
of sound mind when he touched on the Roman Catholic Church.
"Where my château is," he told Morgan and Powel, "there were
churches and chapels. I bought them all and pulled them down to
build my château. I hate churches and priests and masses. You
gentlemen have been in Italy. You have been to Rome. Has not
your blood often boiled to see shoescrapers and porters saying
mass at a place where once a Cicero or Cato and a Scipio have
thundered in elegant harangues to the Roman people?"

At this point he opened his snuffbox for a pinch, revealing
inside the lid a miniature of Frederick.

"Above all authors," he went on, "I admire Newton and Locke.
These opened our eyes to glorious objects and immortal dis-
coveries which we did not think of. One has dissected and laid
open to us the planetary system. The other has, as I may say,
dissected the soul and discovered to us all the powers of the
understanding. On my knees I prostrate all my life before two
such great men as these—to whom I esteem myself as an infant."

The time had now come for the benediction.

"Behold," he said, "two amiable young men, lovers of truth
and inquirers into nature. They are not satisfied with mere appearance, they love investigation and truth, and despise superstition. I command you gentlemen—go on, love truth and search
diligently after it. Hate hypocrisy, masses and above all, hate the
priests."

Morgan could not avoid noticing the chapel that Léonard
Racle designed for the courtyard of the estate—the only church in
the world, as Voltaire often pointed out, dedicated to God.

DEO
EREXIT
VOLTAIRE
MDCCLXI.

This was not all that Morgan noticed. There was a roadside tavern not far away. Scribbled on its walls were these lines:

> *Deo erexit Voltaire.*
> *Behold the pious work of vain Voltaire,*
> *Who never knew a God or said a prayer.*

Our Americans said not a word about Madame Denis. Let us leave her to Madame d'Epinay, who called on Voltaire after seeing much, perhaps too much, of Jean-Jacques Rousseau. "Voltaire's niece is a big joke," she told Diderot's friend Grimm. "Imagine a fat little woman, round as a pumpkin, of about fifty, a real woman, a liar in spite of herself and without meanness, a woman without any wit, although she seems to have some, screaming, putting her foot down, talking politics, trying her hand at verses, a reasoning and an unreasoning woman, without too many pretensions and not really eager to shock anyone. Besides, she likes men: this shows through the self-control she puts on. She adores her uncle, not only as an uncle but as a man. Voltaire idolizes her, makes fun of her, and reveres her."

James Boswell, who knew that he must get around her if he were to get at Voltaire, took pains to write her an obsequious letter on Christmas Day, 1764. "Is it possible, Madame," he asked, "that I may be allowed to lodge one night under the roof of Monsieur de Voltaire? I am a hardy and vigorous Scot. You may mount me to the highest and coldest garret." He would bring his own nightcap. "I would not presume to think of having my head honored with a nightcap of Monsieur de Voltaire."

Having got in, having listened to the master, Boswell did presume, however, to be familiar. "I am sure you were pleased to find a man that gave you no flattery, of which you have had so much that it cannot fail to be insipid or disgusting to you," he wrote Voltaire the next month from Turin. He was not yet finished. "I am diverted," he added a little later, "to see with how little ceremony you treat the soul, altho' you own that you know nothing about it. Many infidels have maintained that ignorance is the mother of devotion . . . It is the soul which has written so many tragedies which adorn the French theater. It is the soul which has surprised us with so much wit against itself, and it is the soul which diffuses kindness and joy over the domains of Ferney. There I have you."

It remained for the Prince de Ligne to take the greatest liberty of all. "The atheists and the deists have never been anything but boring prose writers," he enlightened Voltaire in the summer of 1772. "As for the bombast of Diderot and the dry conversation of d'Alembert, that cold and possibly adroit metaphysician, that is almost enough to turn me into a Capuchin monk . . .

"Horace, Ovid, and Virgil never wrote a word against the gods," he continued. "Only Lucian, really no poet at all, made bad jokes about them. You detested and annihilated the seven or eight atheists at Frederick's court, one of whom so called himself on his calling cards . . .

"The Catholic religion must please anyone inspired with a taste for the fine arts," he argued, thinking of Pergolesi's "Stabat Mater" and Lalande's "Miserere." And having got on this topic, de Ligne could not resist giving his frank opinion of Frederick: "Last year, the great, the very great Frederick told me so many things against God and His saints that really, one day I found his talk too spicy, just like his cuisine which he thinks is first rate because it's the old French cuisine of some farmer-general with no taste buds whatever . . . I shan't end by saying *You must be very stupid, Sir*, but you must be very kind to allow me to go on like this, recalling as you must my respect and my admiration."

Very likely Voltaire was more at ease with Viscount Palmerston, the father of Victoria's prime minister, who surrendered completely to his charm. Said Palmerston: "He is at once the king and the father of the country where he resides, he makes everybody about him happy and he is as good a master of a family as he is a poet. His conversation is enchanting, if he was divided in two and one had to choose between the man one had read and the man one hears, I should be at a loss." Another Englishman who had no complaint to offer—beyond noting that Madame Denis was "a little squat soul . . . strikingly like a smart French commode both in shape and hues"—was the ever so rich and cultivated William Beckford, to whom Voltaire gave his blessing, knowing that he would never try, as did de Ligne, to set him right on the subject of religion.

On this question he was as incorrigible in his old age as he had been in his youth. There was that Easter Sunday when he turned up, escorted by armed guards, in the church he dedicated to God. A day or two earlier he had secured absolution from his sins from an obliging monk; now he proceeded to take communion. This, however, was but an hors-d'oeuvre. He immediately launched into a short sermon to the congregation on the evils of thievery and drunkenness.

"Haul those gallows down!" he is supposed to have cried out at the sight of a crucifix on his lands. This must have been reported to the curé at nearby Moëns, who had the Holy Sacrament removed from Voltaire's church on the ground that it had been profaned. This none too intelligent curé, Philippe Ancian, was quite belligerent, and when a few of his tenants balked at paying their tithes, hired a gang of ruffians to oblige them to behave. This was not all. Ancian, who considered himself responsible for the morals of communicants and noncommunicants alike, took it upon himself to criticize a certain Decroze, whom he caught in the middle of a drunken brawl at the house of Widow Burdet. Her reputation was not of the highest and gossip had it that Ancian was in love with her. There was no denying the fact that Ancian, leading a pack of his followers, knocked Decroze senseless. Here was the priest that Voltaire had been waiting for. "The bishop will know what must be done," he claimed in a letter to the courts. "This priest had the audacity to celebrate mass the next morning, with the host in his murderous hands!" In the end Ancian was let off, but had to acknowledge that Voltaire was providing the money with which his tenants paid their tithes. "He never forgave Voltaire for that!" commented Voltaire's secretary, who may not have been exaggerating.

This was all very exciting. So, in Voltaire's eyes, were the countless tracts he kept publishing to defend the deist point of view. These tracts are not of supreme interest in our time, when a deist is almost as difficult to discover as a druid. To be cruelly accurate, these pamphlets might be dismissed as the work of a bachelor unwilling to accept a hint from a wise woman. Here is the Voltaire who succeeded at times in boring Madame du Deffand.

Perhaps the most earnest of all these tracts is the *Sermon des*

Cinquante (or *Sermon for an Audience of Fifty*) which he released in 1752 and immediately attributed to La Mettrie, the author of *L'Homme Machine*. When read out loud to Frederick at Potsdam, it was earnestly appreciated. Madame du Châtelet should have been pleased by this industrious tribute to her interest in deism, in which there is no trace of Voltaire's wit. And no one would ever guess that this was written by an historian skilled in dealing with facts, pleasant or unpleasant. The fact that mankind has been fascinated for so long by the Last Supper and by its evocation in the service of Holy Communion is dismissed in a manner to please Frederick but very few others. "After three hundred years," Voltaire claims, "they succeeded in having Jesus recognized as a god, and not satisfied with this blasphemy, were so mad as to put this god of theirs in a bit of dough. And while this god is being devoured by mice, they digest him, cast him out in their excrement, and maintain there is no bread in the host, and that God alone has taken the place of the bread . . . They tell us," he goes on, "that people have to have something mysterious, and have to be deceived. Oh! my brothers, how can one commit such an outrage against mankind . . . May this God, the creator of all the worlds, take pity on this sect of Christians who are guilty of blasphemy."

Voltaire was equally vindictive ten years later when he published a supposed condensation of the writings of Jean Meslier, a Roman priest anything but loyal to the Church. To Meslier the "profane" writings of Plato, Xenophon, Cicero, Virgil, and the Emperor Julian were far superior to the books said to have been inspired by God. As for the Jews, they were the most vile and despicable race on earth. Voltaire quoted Meslier as begging God, who was simply outraged by the Christian sect, to bring us all back to Natural Religion, of which Christianity is the declared enemy.

Voltaire was now ready to place on the market his *Republican Ideas*, in which the Christian priesthood was described as an outrage committed against the Gospels. This was immediately followed by the *Catechism of the Normal Man*, in which he made plain that "Detest your enemy like yourself" was the great Christian maxim. He added that he could not imagine that God would appear in the person of a Jew from the lower classes, a Jew condemned to suffer the ultimate indignity. As for himself, he vastly preferred Plato and Socrates.

In the *Dialogue between the Doubter and the Worshiper*, apparently written in 1766, he relented a little, conceding that the real life of Jesus was probably that of a just man who acquired the vices of the Pharisees and whom the Pharisees had killed. Jesus might have rallied his followers around him. The fact that he did not leads us to presume that he preferred to allow the different churches to be indulgent and charitable, with the idea they would unite in recognizing him as their lord and master. At no time did Voltaire express the intention of being kind to the devout. "One must say," he concluded a short essay on the fate of the Calases and the Sirvens, "in praise of our century and in praise of philosophy, that the Calases got their only help in their misfortunes from those wise and educated people who abominate fanaticism. Not a single *devout* person, and I say this regretfully, wiped away their tears or filled their purses."

Not too regretfully. When on this subject, Voltaire could be self-righteous and overemphatic, as in the homage to Viscount Bolingbroke he brought out in 1767. This was not at all what it purported to be—namely, an examination of Bolingbroke's philosophy—but merely another opportunity to deride the morals of the Jews and to dismiss Jesus as a coarse peasant from Judea. He was no more enlightening in *The Count of Boulainvilliers' Dinner*, in which he revealed that at seventy-three he was as revolted as ever by the spectacle of a mass.

The best of Voltaire's deistical reasoning is not be be found in these tracts but in sarcastic flashes from other works. He was the irritating man we have come to respect in the grand row he had with the Président de Brosses, from whom he acquired the life interest in Tournay, the property adjacent to Ferney. De Brosses, who spent his leisure studying the Roman historian Sallust, also gave us the *Lettres Familières Ecrites d'Italie*, which may be described as one of the forgettable travel diaries of the eighteenth century. Perhaps he should never have set out on his Italian journey. In Venice he pronounced Saint Mark's a miserable building and allowed that the palaces were magnificent but tasteless.

For him Vicenza, for all its examples of Palladio, was an ugly and disagreeable town.

Was he saving himself all this time for the quarrel with Voltaire?

The rights to the timber of Tournay were the heart of the matter, as de Brosses might have recognized if he had not been too angry for words. Voltaire is "a very clever fellow with an ugly soul," de Brosses realized in the spring of 1761. "He talks morality, he plays the philosopher, and he has a wicked, a perverse heart." This was a point of view that Voltaire found uncongenial. "You only offered me your friendship," he wrote de Brosses that fall, "in order to poison with lawsuits the end of my life . . . I bought a life interest when I was seventy in that land of yours at Tournay and on the terms you set. I trusted in your honor and your honesty, you dictated the contract, I blindly signed it . . . The fact is that those cords of wood belong to me, and not only those cords but all the timber you have removed from my forest."

De Brosses was ready with an answer. "Please do remember," he wrote, "the prudent advice I gave you as we talked this thing over, when you, reviewing the ups and downs of your career, added that you were naturally of an insolent disposition. I offered you my friendship. The proof that I have not withdrawn this offer is the warning I am giving you once again that you must never write when you are out of your head."

Although Voltaire lost this battle over the cords of wood, he was to prove himself a still respectable enemy in 1770, when de Brosses attempted to join the Academy. This honor was denied after Voltaire pointed out to d'Alembert that de Brosses' character was flawed. "He has," he wrote, "had an ugly lawsuit with me, and I still have the letter in which, with veiled language, he tells me that if I attack him, he'll denounce me as the author of questionable books that I never wrote. I can produce this beautiful evidence for the Academy, and I don't believe that such a man will suit you."

A convenient diversion was the discovery late in 1760 that a grandniece of the great Corneille was living in poverty and obscurity. Voltaire decided to adopt and educate her and so pay his debt to the author of *Le Cid*. This generous impulse did not escape the attention of Fréron. "We must admit," wrote Fréron, "that once she leaves the convent, Mademoiselle Corneille will fall into good hands." Voltaire was already planning a new and correct edition of Corneille's works. This might provide her with a suitable dowry, and also allow the editor to examine a few of the great Corneille's mistakes.

Marie-Françoise Corneille was only sixteen on the day she arrived at Ferney. She had never learned to spell and her conversation indicated that she had seldom been in the best of company. But she had a pretty face, he reported, and her dark eyes were a hundred times more expressive than the last dozen plays of her great-uncle. "She's a cheerful child," wrote Voltaire, "a sensitive thing, gentle, respectable, with the best disposition in the world. It is true that she hasn't yet been able to read her uncle's plays, but you know how quick girls are to learn."

In the meantime the more he read of Corneille, the more critical he became. His *Bérénice*, he told d'Alembert, was detestable. And to another friend he exclaimed: "What execrable trash fifteen or sixteen plays of this great man are! Pradon is another Sophocles in comparison, and Danchet another Euripides!" Here he was referring to two dramatists whose names have vanished from the smaller biographical dictionaries. "How could anyone set this tiresome bore above Racine?" Finally he turned to Madame du Deffand and confessed that Corneille was really disgusting.

When he came to write the commentary on this twelve-volume edition he found verse after verse that made no sense and scolded Corneille for mixing noble with common language in *Le Cid*. However, the job was a commercial success. Catherine insisted on subscribing for fifty copies. All together the crowned heads of Europe put their names down for 864 copies, and 280 noble families accounted for another 545. So £50,000 was on hand for Marie-Françoise's dowry, and he married her off to a captain of the dragoons.

Voltaire could plan a surprise but was himself surprised early in 1768 when the manuscript of his impertinent poem "Guerre Civile de Genève" vanished, to be put into print without his authorization. The first to be accused of the theft was the young critic Jean-François de la Harpe, a guest for the moment. He confessed and was forgiven, but it was obvious that Madame Denis was involved. She was asked to leave Ferney and did so at ten in the morning on the first of March.

Voltaire was desolated. "There is such a thing as destiny, and sometimes destiny is cruel," he wrote her at two that afternoon, knowing that she had set off for Paris. "I went to your door three times, you knocked at mine. I began to walk away my grief in the garden. It was ten o'clock, and I set the needle at ten on the sundial. I was waiting for you to wake up . . . Not a single servant warned me about anything, they all thought I was in the know . . . I realize that it would have been frightful to part from you, but it is even more frightful that you left without seeing me."

"I thought I'd be killed at a quarter of twelve by Monsieur de Voltaire," the secretary Jean-Louis Wagnière informed Madame Denis. "I cried out that you had gone away at ten, and I thought that Father Adam had told him everything. He fell into a horrible rage, but finally calmed down." Wagnière did not have to explain that Father Adam, the unemployed Jesuit hired to let Voltaire win at chess, was not the brightest man at Ferney. Prudently, Wagnière refrained from discussing another, more pressing disagreement with Madame Denis. The trouble was that Voltaire had been insisting that Ferney, although bought in her name, was actually his own property.

The truth about Madame Denis' departure had to be concealed at any cost from Madame du Deffand. "I am seventy-four," Voltaire admitted, "and one sickness after another forces me to keep a strict diet and have plenty of rest. This kind of life can't suit Madame Denis, who was going against her nature to live with me in the country. She had to have one party after another to survive in these horrible deserts, which the Russians say are worse than Siberia for five months of the year."

Madame Denis, who loved money even more than her uncle did, thought she might survive. "In spite of my uncle's whims, I still love him," she wrote a friend. "I'm rather satisfied at the moment by the tone of his letters. But he keeps telling me he wants to be alone. He has added to my small fortune twenty thousand francs a year as long as I stay in Paris. We must let these storms pass over. The wind that drove me away may perhaps bring me back." There were days when she took pity on her benefactor. "The loneliness of the old man makes me shudder," she wrote another friend. "No one knows him better than I do. It's no use his saying he isn't meant for such a life, and if he goes traveling, that will be worse. In spite of his fits of enthusiasm, this man is still interesting to me. He is the one to be pitied. If I weren't born with a warm and grateful heart, I'd be perfectly happy."

In the spring of 1769 Madame Denis was still difficult. "You were born to be cheerful," she told him. "Nature has endowed you with every gift. Don't lose that of being cheerful . . . You reprimanded me for making your house too lively. In the old days that didn't displease you. You know very well that you forced me to leave home."

In the summer she was suggesting that Voltaire was the right man to reconcile Madame du Barry and Choiseul. "If you can accomplish that, people will say that you are a great politician." But she did not forget to remind Voltaire that she had been sent away so that he could live in peace with Father Adam.

In the end a compromise was reached. On the 27th of October 1769 she returned to Ferney, accompanied, as she wished, by a groom, chambermaid, and coachman. In the next spring she was at Voltaire's side when the latest honor descended upon him, a statue by Pigalle commissioned by the wife of Louis XVI's finance minister Jacques Necker. Madame Necker was an earnest woman, as anyone could tell by her description of her husband: "There is something so delicate and so ethereal about his eyes that one is constantly reminded of the painting of an angel." She was not to be defeated in this project.

Subscribers were called for, and subscribers appeared, even though Madame du Deffand hesitated. "If you don't see my name on the list," she told Voltaire, "please believe that my humility is responsible." D'Alembert, however, was truly excited; Pigalle was honored, so was the century. "You know why he is coming to Ferney," said d'Alembert, "and you'll receive him as Virgil would have received Phidias, if Phidias had lived in Virgil's time . . . It's no good your saying that you no longer have any face to offer Monsieur Pigalle. A genius, as long as he is breathing, always has a face."

Trouble came when Jean-Jacques Rousseau insisted on being one of the subscribers. "I have paid dearly enough for the privilege of being allowed this honor," he complained. "You shouldn't refuse his offering," d'Alembert put in, admitting that he had no use for Rousseau. Upon which, Voltaire asked that Rousseau's money be returned. As for Frederick, he had to be on the list, Voltaire thought. "He owes me compensation, as a king, as a philosopher, and as a man of letters. I shan't ask him; you must finish the job. He must give something. Whatever he gives, Madame Denis will give twenty times more."

Frederick not only subscribed but wrote d'Alembert in the ecstatic vein that once was his trademark. "The handsomest monument of Voltaire is that which he has erected himself, in his works. They will last longer than the dome of Saint Peter's, the Louvre and all those buildings which vanity has consecrated to eternity. When the French language is no longer spoken, Voltaire will be translated into the language which will next succeed."

All this would lead one to suspect that the statue was a masterpiece. It was not. It showed Voltaire in the nude, proclaiming that Pigalle knew his anatomy but had forgotten the skill evident in the monument to the Maréchal de Saxe in Strasbourg.

These were the years in which Voltaire turned businessman, promoting the sales all over Europe of watches and stockings produced by his neighbors. Not that he forgot for a second his ties to Versailles. Madame du Barry was not neglected; she might be as serviceable as Madame de Pompadour in communicating with the highest circles. In the summer of 1773, told by the banker LaBorde that she was sending him two kisses, he sent her two of his own with a delicate poem:

Vous ne pouvez empecher cet hommage,
Faible tribut de quiconque a des yeux.
C'est aux mortels d'adorer votre image,
L'original était fait pour les dieux.

[*You cannot prevent this compliment,/A weak tribute for anybody who has eyes./It is up to the mortals to adore your picture,/The original was made for the gods.*]

She replied that this letter sparkled with gaiety. Tibullus himself could not have been more refined or more gallant. So ran the letter composed by her secretary. He sent her a watch manufactured at Ferney.

Like Versailles, Drottningholm must be cultivated. When he learned from Madame du Deffand that Frederick's nephew Gustavus III of Sweden, had been most polite on his visit to Paris, he could barely wait to tell him that the eulogy Gustavus composed for his father drew tears of admiration. "If I am not born your subject," he wrote Gustavus, "my heart tells me that I am." Gustavus, who had the grace to apologize for not calling at Ferney, added "that I am in need of lessons, not praise. . . ." This was not all that Gustavus had to say. Early in 1773 he was moved to another tribute: "Every day I beg the Being of Beings to prolong your days so precious to all mankind and so useful to the progress of reason and of genuine philosophy."

In the Russia of Catherine the Great Voltaire continued to fill the function of a saint, a most benevolent saint. "I am not living in the eighteenth century," he confessed to her in the fall of 1770. "I find I am transported to the Alps at the time of the founding of Babylon." His correspondent in Saint Petersburg was a heroine of the house of Ascanius, brought to the throne of Roxelana. This was one of those timeless compliments: the Ascanians had reigned in her native Anhalt centuries before this, and Roxelana, born a slave, became the sultana of Suleiman II. On reflection he decided that Russia, not Greece, should be considered the birthplace of the arts. "I'm sorry," he went on, "because I like the Greeks in spite of all their faults."

The cult of Voltaire that flourished in Sweden and Russia could not be allowed to wither in Prussia. When Frederick presented him with a porcelain basin in the fall of 1772, he acknowledged the gift with the proper passion. "I knew very well," he wrote, "that Frederick the Great was a better poet than old Kien Long, but I did not know that he was amusing himself in Berlin manufacturing porcelain much superior to that of Kingtehchen, Dresden, and Sèvres. So this astonishing man must eclipse all his rivals in everything he undertakes." This pleasant compliment seems to have produced the most pleasant impression. "As for me," Frederick wrote in the fall of 1773, "I am renouncing war, for fear of incurring the excommunication of the philosophers. I have read the article on war"—this was a reference to the *Encyclopédie*—"and I shuddered."

Since Prussia was so firm in its allegiance, Voltaire may have grieved that the Vatican was so slow to join the all but universal chorus. But he had hopes in Rome. There was always the faithful Cardinal Bernis, who reported in 1771 that Clement XIV, "my dear colleague, has taken your pleasantries very well, both in prose and verse. There is the proof of the superiority of his mind. For as a rule the Italians and the modern Romans don't know what jokes are all about. The Pope would like you to be a trifle more saintly than you are, but he is sincerely flattered by your esteem and wishes you a long life for the sake of literature in our century." This was enough for one day, but not long afterward Bernis was eloquent once again. "They say," he wrote, "that you've written some new verses which are like those you composed in your youth. If that is true, please recall that I am living in the country of Virgil and Horace, but both of them died without heirs. I wish you as long a life as that of Sophocles. No one has a greater claim than you to such a thing."

Voltaire would not have been human if he had not sensed that the time had come for him to assume his rightful position in France. Louis XVI may not have seemed any friendlier than Louis XV—in fact Louis XVI laid plans to seize all of Voltaire's papers the second he was dead or dying, and only retreated from this project in the spring of 1777. But the man who made himself felt in Drottningholm, Saint Petersburg, Potsdam, and even in Rome was not easily disposed of.

On the third of February 1778 Madame Denis set out for Paris, to be followed three days later by Voltaire himself. At eighty-three he was ending his twenty-eight-year exile from the capital. The people of Paris would cheer him, never suspecting that the champion of the Calas family was not exactly a friend of the common man.

As late as 1766 he had his misgivings about anyone who supported himself by physical labor. "I doubt," he said, "that this order of citizens will ever have the time or the capacity to acquire an education. They'd die of hunger before they would turn into philosophers. There is no point in educating the common laborer, we must seek out the bourgeois, the city dweller."

Ten years later his dislike for the lower classes was even more marked in a letter to the Marquis de Condorcet, the believer in the perfectability of man who poisoned himself in 1794 to escape the guillotine. According to Voltaire there were four different kinds of rabble: the rabble who made up the farmers-general, or tax collectors; the rabble who made up the parliament, or corps of legal experts; the rabble in the church; and finally "another rabble to which everything is sacrificed, and this rabble is the common people. Beggared to be sure by the three other rabbles, these are the people who go to mass, vespers, and benediction and for whose benefit we break bread at the altar. And these are the ones for whom LaBarre and Etallonde were condemned as murderers. No one will ever have any trouble in leading this rabble by the halter it has draped around its own neck."

Nor did he have any illusions about a democracy. "As for me," he said, "I prefer an aristocracy. The people are not worthy of governing themselves. I couldn't stand the sight of my wig-maker's posing as a legislator. I'd rather never wear a wig again." A democracy, he thought, was only suitable for a very small country, happily situated.

8

TO BE PUNISHED
AT PARIS

To be punished at Paris was the penalty Voltaire paid for the levity for which he had been so famous for so many years. Suffocated with praise whose insincerity must have been instantly apparent to a master of insincerity like himself, he was even obliged on more than one occasion to wear a crown of laurel wreaths atop his wig. It was all very like a perpetual banquet celebrating the retirement of a none too well loved professor.

Accosted by a customs officer at the frontier, he was already tired and made a tiresome comment. "If you're looking for contraband," he said, "I'm the man they are smuggling into France." He was settled by the tenth of February in an apartment on the rue de Beaune belonging to the Marquis de Villette, a rich man of questionable morals who had seen fit to marry Mademoiselle de Varicourt, one of Voltaire's impoverished neighbors at Ferney.

There came a long line of famous people to the rue de Beaune. Gluck, overlooking Voltaire's lack of enthusiasm for his precursor Rameau, came to pay his respects. So did Marie-Antoinette's favorite, the Comtesse de Polignac, Madame du Barry, Madame Necker, and Balbastre, the musician taken up by the Choiseuls at Chanteloup. Finally, there was Benjamin Franklin, for whom he staged the type of performance that went over so well at Ferney. After making a few excuses for his English —"I yielded for a moment," he apologized, "to the vanity of speaking the same language as Mr. Franklin"—he gave his blessing: *God and Liberty* to Franklin's fifteen-year-old grandson.

Madame du Deffand, who had no respect for either Madame Denis or the Marquise de Villette, hesitated for a time to make her appearance, although Voltaire had the courtesy to send her a charming note. "I arrive a dead man," he told her, "and I only want to come back to life to throw myself at the feet of Madame du Deffand." "Perhaps I'll go and see him some time," she wrote Horace Walpole. "I'm not sure when. I'm afraid to meet all the fakes that cluster around him. However, I want to be on good terms with him." Later she said: "If he looks me up, I'll see him with pleasure. If he drops me, what do I care?" At last, on April 12, Voltaire called on her. "I finally had my visit from Voltaire," she told Walpole. "I put him at his ease. He stayed for an hour and was infinitely charming. People call him the *Calas man*. If he sees me often, I shall be pleased. If he lets me alone, I'll get along. I no longer have any desires or any plans. The honors he has been receiving are ineffable."

On call was Voltaire's Genevan doctor Théodore Tronchin, who saw no need to adopt a bedside manner, even though it was obvious that the patient was dying, among other ailments, of a strangury, the painful discharge, drop by drop, of his urine. "The way things are going," Tronchin told the Marquis de Villette, "his strength is going fast, and we shall be the witnesses if not the accomplices of Voltaire's death." The doctor was resigned and irritated. "If he dies cheerfully, as he promised, I'll be mistaken," he told another member of the Tronchin family. "He'll drift away with his cowardice. I believe he is really worried by his approaching end. I bet you he won't joke about it." Later on Tronchin observed: "I've seen a lot of madmen in my life, but never anyone more insane than he. He really thinks he's going to live to be a hundred." Still later he was positive that Voltaire would never be missed. "People are already estimating all the harm he has done society . . . What astonishes me not a little is that this estimate is being made by what one calls fashionable people."

Since all of Voltaire's plays, with the exception of the comedy

Nanine, dating from 1748, had disappeared from the repertory of the Comédie Française, he was understandably anxious for the success of his latest, *Irène*, which had been performed the year before at Ferney for the marriage of the Marquis de Villette. Madame Denis is said to have wept at the first production, but this did not prevent her from approving this time any number of unauthorized changes in the text. This did not improve Voltaire's disposition. Neither did the death of LeKain, one of his favorite actors. He was scheduled for the role of the hermit Léonce, Irene's father, in this pageant of Constantinople in the days of the Emperor Alexius Comnenus.

A revival of *Irène* in the twentieth century does not seem imminent; Voltaire was shrewd in admitting that he failed to attain perfection. "I am taking the liberty," he told the French Academy, "of begging you to reprimand me for the faults I have committed . . . Old age passes for being incorrigible, but I, gentlemen, believe that one must try to improve oneself at the age of one hundred . . . I was the first to extract a little gold out of the mud in which the genius of Shakespeare had been plunged by his century."

Whether *Irène* was a masterpiece or a disaster was quite unimportant. The savior of the Calas family was the man of the hour. This was evident at the dress rehearsal on March 14: public opinion had decided that the play could not fail. Voltaire himself was too feeble to be on hand, but Madame Denis was there, as was Marie-Antoinette, who had stolen away from the supervision of her husband. "Ah, ah, Monsieur de Voltaire is in Paris, but without my permission," Louis XVI insisted. His brother, the Comte d'Artois, the future Charles X, had to be on hand; he believed he was the last word and had recently won a bet with Marie-Antoinette that his palace in the Bois would be completed in sixty days. Not that Artois was devoted to Voltaire. Ten years before this, he greeted a rumor that he was dead by observing: "A great man has just died, and a great scoundrel."

But with the sixth performance of *Irène*, Artois dispatched a captain of his guards to congratulate Voltaire, who elected this time to appear in person. He no sooner reached his box than the crowd screamed: "The crown!" Upon which one of the actors placed a crown of laurels on his head. "My God! Do you want to kill me with glory!" he cried out, literally strangled—so it was said—with tears of joy. He passed the crown on to the Marquise de Villette, but the public insisted it belonged to the "French Sophocles." The Marquise agreed, Voltaire objected, and finally the Prince de Beauvau returned the crown to the victim. According to Diderot's faithful German friend, Friedrich Melchior Grimm, the delirium of the crowd did not subside for a full twenty minutes. "The enthusiasm with which the apotheosis of Voltaire in his lifetime has been celebrated," Grimm concluded, "is the just recompense not only for the wonders of his genius but also for the happy revolution he has brought about in the mind and morals of his century. Combating prejudice in every order of society, he has bestowed more dignity on the literary profession and spread the power of opinion, ensuring its independence from all other powers save genius and reason." Grimm's ecstasy was unfeigned, even if hard to unravel. "As a rule, revolutions are quite charming," he maintained, although he did find it convenient to sit out the French Revolution in Germany.

But Voltaire was not yet done with laurel wreaths. When he visited the Masonic Lodge of the Nine Sisters, he was presented with yet another crown and forced to listen to a discourse in which it was argued that he had not only erected a temple to the Supreme Being but provided an asylum for deserving outlaws. "Dear brother," he was told, "you were a Freemason before we admitted you, and you did your duty before you assumed that obligation at our hands."

The ceremony at the French Academy was less formidable, since fifty per cent of the immortals stayed away, true either to their clerical robes or to their clerical sentiments. Under these circumstances, Voltaire may have been wise to strike a noncontroversial attitude. To his august peers he proposed they all join forces to produce a new, supposedly definitive dictionary of the French language. The etymology of every word would be studied, a decent attention would be paid to the conjugation of unfamiliar irregular verbs, and citations from authors of real standing would be supplied. To prove his own generosity, he offered to assume full responsibility for the letter A. This would have been a lamentable waste of time if Voltaire at eighty-three had anything left to contribute to French literature. Doubtless, he hadn't. In self-defense he might have claimed that the boring assignment he was undertaking was unexpected from a troublemaker of his reputation.

The one undoubted favor that Voltaire did posterity by coming to Paris was consenting to pose for Jean-Antoine Houdon, the peerless sculptor of the famous in the late eighteenth century. It is thanks to Houdon that we may imagine the arrogance of John Paul Jones, the craftiness of Franklin, the sincerity of Jefferson, not to mention the serenity of Washington and the madness of Rousseau. No one can argue with his representations of Voltaire, whether one is referring to the seated figure in the Comédie Française, the standing figure in the Panthéon, or the numerous busts.

Honest John Adams was a naïve observer compared to Houdon, but admitted he was fascinated by the glimpse he caught of Voltaire attending a revival of his old play *Alzire*. "Although," said Adams, "he was very far advanced in age, had the paleness of death and deep lines and wrinkles in his face, he had at some times an eager, piercing stare, and at others a sparkling vivacity in his eyes. They were still the poet's eyes with a fine frenzy rolling."

As long as the frenzy rolled, Voltaire would worry the Roman Catholic Church and be worried himself about being buried with dignity. Would he be tossed into a common sewer? This was preying on his mind when he consented on February 21 to receive Abbé Gaultier from the church of Saint-Sulpice. "He's a nice imbecile," Voltaire remarked having made his confession to Gaultier on March 2. While refusing to pass for a Catholic, he said he wished to die in the Roman Catholic faith. He could not deny his works, he admitted, but if ever he scandalized the Church, he begged God's forgiveness and that of the Church as well. Taking communion, however, was out of the question: he was spitting too much blood for that. All this was ultimately embarrassing to Abbé Gaultier, who was reminded by the archbishop that he had exceeded his powers.

Perhaps the closest Voltaire came to making a proper confession was when he talked to his secretary Wagnière. "I die," he told Wagnière, "worshiping God, loving my friends, not hating my enemies, and detesting superstition."

But Abbé Gaultier had his hopes. "You must be convinced, sir," he wrote him, "that I am sending my prayers to heaven for your true happiness. You can have no doubt about my feelings toward you. If you allow me to pay you a call, I shall take the liberty of telling you out loud what I dare not set down in a letter dictated far more by my mind." To this Voltaire replied that he would be happy to see Languet's successor, the curé of Saint-Sulpice, and when back in good health, Gaultier himself.

The curé of Saint-Sulpice and the abbé did make their appearance in his bedroom in the evening of May 30. But they were too late to enter into a rewarding conversation. Voltaire died between the hours of eleven and twelve, his last breath hurried by the tincture of opium recommended by the imperious Duc de Richelieu. The story has come down that the curé of Saint-Sulpice begged him in his last moments to recognize the divinity of Jesus Christ. "In God's name, don't mention him to me!" Voltaire is said to have murmured. According to another version, his last words were: "Let me die in peace!"

The body was promptly embalmed under the supervision of Madame Denis' nephew Abbé Mignot, who hoped against hope that Voltaire might be given Christian burial, despite the reluctance of the curé of Saint-Sulpice. On the next day the corpse was stuffed into a dressing gown, the night cap was stuck on his wig, and a coach rolled out from Paris in the direction of the Abbey of Scellières in Champagne, where Mignot planned to inter the remains. Not all the remains, however. The heart of Voltaire was snatched by the Marquis de Villette, the brain by the pharmacist Mitouart. The whereabouts of the heart and brain are unknown today. As for the remains minus heart and brain, they too have disappeared. The corpse was deposited in the choir of the ruined abbey and a low mass celebrated in Voltaire's honor. But all this was illegal; the curé of Saint-Sulpice protested; the prelate of neighboring Troyes agreed. And it was obvious to everyone concerned that the churchmen near Ferney would have opposed Voltaire's desire to be buried in hallowed ground on his property.

Eventually, the corpse at Scellières was transported to the Panthéon in Paris. Here, too, no peace. In 1814, on the collapse of the Empire, the Panthéon was invaded and Voltaire's remains— like those of Rousseau—scattered no one knows where.

Madame Denis, who sold off Voltaire's small library with his marginal notes to Catherine the Great, and disposed of Ferney for £230,000 to the Marquise de Villette, disappeared from history about the time she said she wished Ferney might be burned to the ground. She then married a certain Duvivier, a captain of the dragoons who seems to have been less her husband than her tyrant.

Voltaire will never disappear from history. It seems safe, however, in 1981 to declare that he was loyal only to himself, and that the self was subject to change without notice. Like an accomplished double agent, he took all the precautions imaginable, and it is wise to remember that this anti-Christian had his firm friends in the Roman Catholic Church. He could count on at least two popes to bless his intentions, and it may be that in the other world the Cardinal de Bernis is still looking forward to reading a few poems worthy of his reputation.

At the risk of annoying bigoted Roman Catholics and equally bigoted agnostics, deists, and atheists, the point must be made that he was not a solemn man. This will contradict the opinion of historians who have taken the Enlightenment so seriously that they talk on about the benevolent despots of the eighteenth century. One representative of this point of view was Thomas Carlyle, who could find almost no fault with Frederick the Great. Another was Gladstone's admirer John Morley, positive that the Roman Catholic Church in the eighteenth century was "a monster sodden with black corruption, with whom in the breast of humane man there could be no terms." To be fair to Carlyle and Morley, it must be admitted that their books were designed for the audience quite satisfied with the success of the German Empire under Bismarck. And if Bismarck was a genius, it was good to point out that the triumph of Bismarck's William I was prepared by Voltaire's old acquaintance Frederick the Great.

Voltaire could be occasionally sincere, as in his portrait of Louis XIV. What he thought of Frederick may be guessed by anyone who opens the slender volume, *Mémoires pour Servir à la Vie de Monsieur de Voltaire, Ecrits par Lui-même.* Here is no portrait of a philanthropist. Fascinated but not exactly mesmerized by the personality of this singular Prussian, Voltaire studied his behavior with the care a scientist might devote to the habits of a serpent.

ACKNOWLEDGMENTS
& BIBLIOGRAPHY

I am very grateful to Goldwin Smith of the Wayne State University history department for reading my manuscript so carefully, and am also thankful for the suggestions of Professor Richard D. Miles, the Reverend Julien Gunn of Nashville, and the Reverend Richard W. Ingalls of Detroit.

Of all the books listed in this bibliography the most provocative is René Pomeau's *La Religion de Voltaire*.

Aldington, Richard: *Voltaire*. London, 1925.
Aldridge, A. Owen. *Voltaire and the Century of Light*. Princeton, 1975.
Arnason, H. H. *The Sculpture of Houdon*. New York, 1975.
Assé, Eugene, ed. *Madame de Graffigny: Lettres*. Geneva, 1972.

Babelon, André, ed. *Diderot: Lettres á Sophie Volland*. 2 vols., Paris, 1938.
Bachaumont, Louis Petit de. *Mémoires*. 36 vols., London, 1779–89.
Baléou, Jean. *Fréron Contre les Philosophes*. Geneva, 1975.
Bangert, William V., S. J. *A History of the Society of Jesus*. Saint Louis, 1972.
Barbier, E.-J.-F. *Journal Historique et Anecdotique du Règne de Louis XV*, 4 vols., Paris, 1847.
Becker, Carl L. *The Heavenly City of the Eighteenth-Century Philosophers*. New Haven, 1930.
Berl, Emmanuel, *et al.*, eds. *Voltaire: Mélanges*. Paris, 1961.

Bertrand, Joseph. *D'Alembert.* Paris, 1889.

Besterman, Theodore. *Voltaire.* New York, 1969.

———, ed. *Lettres d'Amour de Voltaire à Sa Nièce.* Paris, 1957.

———, ed. *Lettres de la Marquise du Châtelet.* 2 vols., Geneva, 1956.

———, ed. *Notebooks of Voltaire.* 2 vols., Toronto, 1960.

———, ed. *Voltaire: Correspondance.* 107 vols., Geneva, 1953–65.

Bien, David D. *The Calas Affair.* Princeton, 1960.

Billy, André, ed. *Diderot: Oeuvres.* Paris, 1946.

Bluche, François, *et al. Voltaire.* Paris, 1978.

Boiteau, Paul, ed. *Mémoires de Madame d'Epinay.* 2 vols., Paris, 1884.

Braun, Théodore-E.-D. *Un Ennemi de Voltaire: Le Franc de Pompignan.* Paris, 1972.

Brenner, Jacques, ed. *Mémoires pour Servir à la Vie de Monsieur de Voltaire, Ecrits par Lui-même.* Paris, 1965.

Brookner, Anita. *Greuze: The Rise and Fall of an Eighteenth Century Phenomenon.* Greenwich, 1972.

Buchdal, Gerd. *The Image of Newton and Locke in the Age of Reason.* London, 1961.

Caillois, Roger, ed. *Montesquieu: Oeuvres Complètes.* 2 vols., Paris, 1939.

Cantacuzène, Charles-Adolphe, ed. *Collection des Plus Belles Pages du Prince de Ligne.* Paris, 1934.

Carlyle, Thomas. *History of Frederick II of Prussia.* 10 vols., London, 1858–75.

Carré, Henri. *La Marquise de Pompadour.* Paris, 1933.

———. *Le Règne de Louis XV.* Paris, 1911.

Carrère, Casimir. *Les Amours Scandaleuses du Maréchal-Duc de Richelieu.* Paris, 1980.

Caussy, Fernand. *Voltaire Seigneur de Village.* Paris, 1912.

Cheke, Marcus. *The Cardinal de Bernis.* New York, 1958.

Cobham, Alfred, ed. *The Eighteenth Century: Europe in the Age of the Enlightenment.* New York, 1969.

Cohen, I. Bernard. *Franklin and Newton.* Philadelphia, 1956.

Colomb, M.-R., ed. *Le Président de Brosses en Italie: Lettres Familières Ecrites d'Italie en 1739 et 1740.* 2 vols., Paris, 1858.

Daval, Pierre. *La Musique en France au Dix-huitième Siècle.* Paris, 1961.

DeBeer, Sir Gavin, ed., *Voltaire's British Visitors* (Vol. 4, *Studies on Voltaire and the Eighteenth Century*). Geneva, 1957.

Delattre, André. *Voltaire L'Impétueux.* Paris, 1957.

Desfontaines, Guyot. *La Voltairomanie*. Paris, 1738.

Desnoiresterres, Gustave LeBrusoys. *Voltaire et la Société du Dix-huitième Siècle*. 8 vols., Paris, 1871–76.

Dieckmann, H., and Sezneck, Jean, eds. *Diderot-Falconet Correspondance*. Frankfurt, 1956.

Dobson, Austin. *Horace Walpole: A Memoir*. London, 1927.

Donvez, Jacques. *De Quoi Vivait Voltaire?*. Paris, 1959.

Doscot, Gérard, *Madame du Deffand ou le Monde où l'on s'ennuie*, Lausanne, 1967.

——, ed. *Mémoires de Madame de Staal-Delaunay*. Paris, 1970.

Dussieux, I., and Soulié, Eud., eds. *Mémoires du Duc de Luynes sur la Cour de Louis XV*. 14 vols., Paris, 1860–66.

Duvernet, Théophile-Imarigeon. *Vie de Voltaire*. London, 1786.

D'Estrée, Paul. *Le Maréchal de Richelieu*. Paris, n.d.

Faure, Edgar. *La Banqueroute de Law*. Paris, 1977.

Fleischauer, Charles, ed. *Frederick the Great: L'Anti-Machiavel* (Vol. 5, *Studies on Voltaire and the Eighteenth Century*). Geneva, 1958.

Fuchs, M., ed. *Rousseau: Lettre à d'Alembert sur les Spectacles*. Geneva, 1948.

Gagnebin, Bernard, and Raymond, Marcel, eds. *Rousseau: Oeuvres Complètes*. 4 vols., Paris, 1964–67.

Gay, Peter. *The Enlightenment*. 2 vols., New York, 1966–69.

——. *Voltaire's Politics*. Princeton, 1959.

Gide, André. *Journal 1889–1939*. Paris, 1965.

——. *Journal 1939–1949: Souvenirs*. Paris, 1966.

Glotz, Marguerite, and Maire, Madeleine. *Salons du Dix-huitième Siècle*. Paris, 1949.

Goncourt, Edmond and Jules. *Sophie Arnould*. Paris, 1922.

——. *La Du Barry*. Paris, 1952.

——. *La Duchesse de Châteauroux et Ses Soeurs*. Paris, 1935.

——. *La Femme au Dix-huitième Siècle*. Paris, 1938.

——. *Histoire de Marie-Antoinette*. Paris, 1925.

——. *Madame de Pompadour*. Paris, 1927.

——. *Portraits Intimes du Dix-huitième Siècle*. 2 vols., Paris, 1924.

Gooch, C.P. *Louis XV: The Monarchy in Decline*. London, 1956.

Groos, René, ed. *Voltaire: Romans et Contes*. Paris, 1950.

Guéhenno, Jean. *Jean-Jacques*. 2 vols., Paris, 1962.

Guillemin, Henri. *Un Homme, Deux Ombres*. Paris, 1943.

Guimbaud, Louis. *Saint-Non et Fragonard*. Paris, 1928.

Hadley, William, ed. *The Letters of Horace Walpole*. London, 1939.

Hamilton, Earl J., "The Political Economy of France at the Time of John Law," *History of Political Economy*. Vol 1., November 1969.

Hansford Johnson, Pamela, ed. *The Misfortunate Margravine: Early Memoirs of Wilhelmina*. London, 1970.

Helvétius, Claude-Adrien. *De l'Esprit*. The Hague, 1759.

Holbach, Paul-Henry Thiry, Baron d'. *Système Social*. London, 1773.

Hubert, René. *Holbach et Ses Amis*. Paris, 1928.

Hyde, H. Montgomery. *John Law*. London, 1969.

Ilchester, Earl of, and Mrs. Langford-Brooke. *The Life of Sir Charles Hanbury Williams*. London, 1929.

James, William. *The Varieties of Religious Experience*. New York, n.d.

Jefferson, Thomas, ed. *The Life and Morals of Jesus of Nazareth*. Washington, 1904.

Ketton-Cramer, R. W. *Horace Walpole*. London, 1940.

Kors, Alan Charles. *D'Holbach's Coterie*. Princeton, 1976.

Kramick, Isaac. *Bolingbroke and His Circle*. Cambridge, 1968.

Lanson, Gustave. *Voltaire*. Paris, 1906.

Lescure, M. de, ed. *Journal et Mémoires de Mathieu Marais*. 4 vols., Paris, 1862.

Leuridant, Félicien, ed. *Prince de Ligne: Fragments de l'Histoire de Ma Vie*. 2 vols., Paris, 1927.

Levitine, George. *The Sculpture of Falconet*. Greenwich, 1972.

Lewis, Wilmarth Sheldon. *Horace Walpole*. New York, 1960.

—— and Smith, Warren Hunting, eds. *Horace Walpole's Correspondence with Madame du Deffand*. 6 vols., New Haven, 1939.

Ligne, Charles-Joseph, Prince de. *Mémoires et Lettres*. Paris, 1923.

Longchamp, Sébastien. *Mémoires sur Voltaire*. 2 vols., Paris, 1926.

Lough, J., ed. *The Encyclopédie of Diderot and d'Alembert*. Cambridge, 1954.

Mabee, Charles, "Thomas Jefferson's Anti-Clerical Bible," *Historical Magazine of the Protestant Episcopal Church*. December 1979.

Martin, Marietta. *Une Française à Varsovie en 1766: Madame Geoffrin*. Paris, 1936.

Masson, Frédéric, ed. *Mémoires et Lettres de François-Joachim de Pierre, Cardinal de Bernis*. 2 vols., Paris, 1903.

155

Maugras, Gaston. *Le Duc et la Duchesse de Choiseul*. Paris, 1903.
——. *La Cour de Lunéville au Dix-huitième Siècle*. Paris, 1904.
——. *Dernières Années de la Cour de Lunéville*. Paris, 1922.
Maurois, André. *Voltaire*. New York, 1938.
May, Maija M. *Comte d'Argental* (Vol. 76, *Studies on Voltaire and the Eighteenth Century*). Geneva, 1970.
Micha, Hugues, ed. *Voltaire d'après Sa Correspondance avec Madame Denis*. Paris, 1972.
Mitford, Nancy. *Frederick the Great*. New York, 1970.
——. *Madame de Pompadour*. New York, 1965.
——. *Voltaire in Love*. New York, 1957.
Moland, Louis-Emile-Dieudonné, ed. *Voltaire: Oeuvres Complètes*. 52 vols., Paris, 1877–85.
Monselet, Charles. *Fréron, ou l'Illustre Critique*. Paris, 1864.
Morley, John. *Voltaire*. London, 1886.
Mornet, Danuel, *La Pensée Française au Dix-huitième Siècle*. Paris, 1926.

Naves, Raymond. *Le Goût de Voltaire*. Paris, 1936.
——. *Voltaire et l'Encyclopédie*. Paris, 1938.
Nolhac, Pierre de. *François Boucher, Premier Peintre du Roi*. Paris, 1907.
——. *Louis XV et Marie Leczinska*. Paris, 1928.
Norton, Lucy. *First Lady of Versailles*. London, 1978.
Noyes, Alfred. *Voltaire*. New York, 1936.

Orieux, Jean. *Voltaire*. Paris, 1966.

Perry, Norma. *Sir Everard Fawkener, Friend and Correspondent of Voltaire* (Vol. 83, *Studies on Voltaire and the Eighteenth Century*). Oxford, 1975.
Pomeau, René. "La Confession et la Mort de Voltaire," *Revue d'Histoire Littéraire de la France*. July-September 1955.
——. *La Religion de Voltaire*. Paris, 1956.
——. ed. *Voltaire par Lui-Même*. Paris, 1968.
——. ed. *Voltaire: Oeuvres Historiques*. Paris, 1957.
Pottle, Frederick A., ed. *Boswell on the Grand Tour*. New York, 1964.

Quennell, Peter. *Alexander Pope: The Education of a Genius*. New York, 1968.
Quintana, Ricardo, ed. *Gulliver's Travels and Other Writings by Jonathan Swift*. New York, 1958.

Rathery, E.-J.-B., ed. *Journal et Mémoires du Marquis d'Argenson.* 9 vols., Paris, 1859.

Réau, Louis. *Etienne-Maurice Falconet.* 2 vols., Paris, 1922.

———. *Biographie Critique de Houdon.* Paris, 1935.

———. *Jean-Baptiste Pigalle.* Paris, 1950.

Retzler, Marta. *Voltaire and the Encyclopedia* (Vol. 30, *Studies on Voltaire and the Eighteenth Century*). Geneva, 1964.

Richelieu, Louis-François-Armand de Plessis. *Mémoires.* Paris, 1855.

Ridgeway, R. S. *Voltaire and Sensibility.* Montreal, 1973.

Riding, Laura. *Voltaire.* London, 1927.

Rightman, Jack. *Adrienne Lecouvreur. The Actress and the Age.* Englewood Cliffs, 1971.

Ritter, Gerhard. *Friedrich der Grosse.* Heidelberg, 1954.

Rousseau, André-Michel. *Voltaire et l'Angleterre* (Vols. 145–47, *Studies on Voltaire and the Eighteenth Century*). 3 vols., London, 1976.

Saint-André, Claude. *Le Régent.* Paris, 1928.

Saint-Aulaire, Marquis de, ed. *Correspondance Inédite de Madame du Deffand.* 2 vols., Paris, 1859.

Sainte-Beuve, Charles-Augustin de. "Voltaire et le Président de Brosses," *Causeries du Lundi,* Vol. 7, Paris, 1928.

Schwarzbach, Bertram Eugene. *Voltaire's Old Testament Criticism.* Geneva, 1971.

Seznec, Jean, and Ashémar, Jean. *Diderot: Salons.* 4 vols., London, 1960.

Shellabarger, Samuel. *Lord Chesterfield.* London, 1935.

Simon, Edith. *The Making of Frederick the Great.* London, 1963.

Sitwell, Edith. *Alexander Pope.* London, 1930.

Strachey, Lytton. *Biographical Essays.* London, 1948.

———. *Landmarks in French Literature.* London, 1949.

———. *Literary Essays.* London, 1948.

Torrey, Norman L. *The Spirit of Voltaire.* New York, 1938.

———. *Voltaire and the English Deists.* New Haven, 1930.

Tourneux, Maurice, ed. *Correspondance Littéraire, Philosophique et Critique par Grimm et al.* 16 vols., Paris, 1877–82.

Trabucco, Joseph, ed. *Madame du Deffand: Lettres à Voltaire.* Paris, 1922.

Tronchin, Henry. *Le Conseiller François Troncgin et Ses Amis.* Paris, 1883.

Truc, Gonzague, ed. *Saint-Simon: Mémoires.* 8 vols., Paris, 1947–65.

Truchet, Jacques, ed. *Le Théâtre du Dix-huitième Siècle.* 2 vols., Paris, 1974.

Van Doren, Carl. *Swift*. New York, 1930.

Vartarian, Ara, ed. *La Mettrie's L'Homme Machine*. Princeton, 1960.

Vergniol, C. and Audéat, P., eds. *Madame du Hausset, Mouffle d'Angerville: La Marquise de Pompadour*. Paris, 1927.

Verlet, Pierre, ed. *Les Ebénistes du Dix-huitième Siècle Français*. Paris, 1963.

Vernière, Paul, ed. *Diderot: Oeuvres Esthétiques*. Paris, 1953.

Wade, Ira O. *The Intellectual Development of Voltaire*. Princeton, 1969.

——. *Voltaire and Madame du Châtelet*. Princeton, 1941.

Weinschenker, Anne Betty. *Falconet, His Writings and His Friend Diderot*. Geneva, 1966.

Wilburn, R., ed. *John Locke: An Essay Concerning Human Understanding*. London, 1947.

Wildenstein, George. *The Paintings of Fragonard*. London, 1960.

Williams, David, ed. *Voltaire: Commentaires sur Corneille*. 3 vols., Danbury, 1974.

Wilson, Arthur N. *Diderot*. New York, 1972.

Wirz, Charles. "Cinq Lettres et un Poème de Voltaire," *Musée de Genève*. No. 167, July 1976.

INDEX

159